The People's
True Tales of Blyth ... and other places

by

Jim Harland

Previous page: *While working for the Blyth News in 1958 the author was sent to Ashington to cover a recording of the Wilfred Pickles BBC Radio show Have A Go. Little did he know, when larking about in front of the microphones, that some twenty-two years later he would be a full-time employee of the BBC. The radio show listened to by hundreds of thousands had a popular catch phrase said to the successful competitors by Wilfred – 'Give him/her the money Barney.' The 'Barney' was producer Barney Colehan, later to produce the Good Old Days television programme from the City of Varieties in Leeds. The pianist of Have A Go was Violet Carlson, later to achieve national fame as Ena Sharples in Coronation Street.*

Front cover, centre picture: *Mike Neville in Spartans garb with Terry Johnson (left) and Dave Clarke at the outdoor reception at Broadcasting House before their FA Cup tie at Wrexham.*

Copyright © Jim Harland 2002

First published in 2002 by

The People's History Ltd
Suite 1, Byron House
Seaham Grange Business Park
Seaham, Co. Durham
SR7 0PY

ISBN 1 902527 97 6

No part of this publication may be reproduced, stored in a mechanical retrieval system, or transmitted, in any form or by any means, electronic, mechanical, photocopying, recording or otherwise, without prior permission of the author.

Contents

Introduction		4
Acknowledgements		6
1.	Memories	7
2.	We Grow By Industry	19
3.	The Royal, The Roxy and Cinemas	27
4.	Operatic Societies	37
5.	The Entertainers	61
6.	The Red Shadow	69
7.	A Career In Journalism And Broadcasting	77
8.	Sport	103
9.	And Finally ... Music, Music, Music	123

Thank you for buying this book, *True Tales of Blyth ... and other places*. To see the latest range of books available in The People's History series, and a selection of historical prints we have on offer, please visit our website:

www.thepeopleshistory.co.uk

Introduction

Jim Harland was born in Blyth in 1935 and, apart from two brief spells, has lived his entire life in the town. After being educated locally and at Skerry's College, Newcastle, started a career in journalism with the *Morpeth Herald* at the age of sixteen. That career took him to the *Blyth News* (twice) the *Cambridge Evening News*, the Cambridge Freelance and General News Service, the *Newcastle Chronicle & Journal* (three times), the *Sunday Mirror* and eventually into television with BBC *Look North* and radio journalism as sports producer for Radio Newcastle. He took early retirement in 1989 but has continued on a part-time basis as a freelance soccer commentator on national television and the Internet.

Jim, as chairman of Blyth Youth Council, was in the first party of young people to visit the twin town of Solingen in Germany returning fourteen years later to sing the lead in an operatic show. He was an active member of the Blyth Phoenix and Cambois Dramatic Societies, first secretary, later leading man and producer, of the reformed Blyth Operatic Society, captain and chairman of Blyth Cricket Club, a Class One referee in local football and the person responsible for launching the highly popular Blyth Town Fair which takes over the town centre every July.

When the Wallaw Cinema, the only one left in the town, was threatened with closure he managed it for eighteen months on behalf of a Scottish company and is still actively involved in the cinema as a member of the Future of the Wallaw Group. Jim is married and lives with his wife, Rosemary, in Blyth. They have two daughters, Janet and Alison, both talented singers who have sung the leads in shows in the town. Alison, in recent years, played opposite Jim in *Annie* and *Sweeney Todd* – both staged at the Wallaw.

The author interviews Kevin Keegan.

Pupils of Crofton Junior School staged Alice in Wonderland as the annual production in 1972 in which the author's eldest daughter, Janet (seated to the left of the teacher) played Alice. It was to lead to principal roles at Ridley High School and with the Blyth Phoenix Theatre group in My Fair Lady and Barnum. Janet is now a teacher herself producing shows at Guide Post Middle School.

In May 1979, pupils of the Princess Louise Middle School, Blyth, put on a production of operetta The Fire Maid despite the frustration of the teacher-producer Michael Pritchard at the lack of boys coming forward for audition. The show marked the first appearance on stage of Alison Harland (holding the stick), the author's youngest daughter who has since taken starring roles for both the Blyth and Beaconsfield Operatic Societies.

Acknowledgements

I am eternally grateful to my mother, Emily, and the following for their assistance in providing pictures, information, particularly names, and putting me right on certain facts:

Jack Allen, Jim Bell, Gilbert Barker, Jimmy Craft, Pauline Dean, Susan Dixon, Alf Douglas, Doreen Douglas, Bill Elliott, Gerry Evans, Brian Graysmark, Trevor Harder, Bill 'Pop' Long, Madge & Christine McSherry, Neil and Bill Mitcheson, George Nairn, Alan Pitkeathly, Edna Riddell, Peter Robertson, Alan Roughead, Gordon Smith, Bill Thompson and Joan Waddle.

And last and most certainly not least, my wife, Rosemary, for her coffee, proof reading and putting up with my single-mindedness while compiling this book.

Rosemary Harland, wife of the author, is seen here flanked by her sisters Joyce and Diana as they prepared to take part in a 1940 show at the Hartford Welfare Hall. They are the daughters of the late Dr William Brown, the GP for the Cramlington area for twenty-six years up to his death in 1954.

MEMORIES

The author was named after an uncle, James Davison Harland, who was killed during the First World War. His name is inscribed on the War Memorial, which stands in Ridley Park, Blyth and also on the 1914-18 Wall Memorial in the entrance to St Cuthbert's Church.

The horse and cart on which I sat alongside the driver was taking our furniture, my Mum and Dad and older brother Frank away from the two-bedroom terraced house in Salisbury Street where I had lived for four of my five years. It was moving us to Garden City – the sprawling new council estate of semi-detached houses with original names such as First Avenue, Second Avenue and so on until they stopped at Twenty-sixth Avenue. The title of Garden City came about because the houses had gardens front and back and there were privet hedges in abundance for privacy.

Eighty-nine Salisbury Street was where I had my first memory. It was one Christmas morning when my brother and I came downstairs to find out what Santa had brought us. It was a monster fort complete with soldiers and searchlights. Dad worked as a labourer at Bates Pit and there was no spare money to buy us gifts. So as not to disappoint us he spent months in secret building the fort himself.

The second memory I recall was of a lie I told after I had started Wright Street Infants School just at the outbreak of the Second World War. I was just four at the time. In those days there were no school lunches and children went home at the dinner break and returned in the afternoon. On this occasion our teacher, I cannot recall her name, opened the afternoon session by getting her pupils to stand up one by one and say what they had been given for lunch. It was very interesting and when it came to my turn I can remember saying I had a number of vegetables, beef, pork and ham. The teacher asked me again and I repeated what I had said to the best of my ability. She asked me again

Emily Harland, the mother of the author, now in her 90th year, is pictured right with her brothers and sisters. From left to right: Billy, who was killed in the Second World War, Maude, Margaret, Albie, who was captured by the Germans in Crete and spent the war a prisoner in Germany.

and got the same answer. It was then she told me to go and get my brother Frank from his classroom. He duly came and when asked what we had been served for lunch replied, 'Bread and jam.' He was told to return to his class and I was told to sit down.

We were travelling to Twentieth Avenue by horse and cart because that was the way the working class moved home in 1940. In fact horse travel was so prevalent my dad was able to get as much manure as he wanted for his gardens by just taking his shovel and pail out into the road. Number 80, Twentieth Avenue, was a palace compared to what we had left. No longer did we have to dash to the bottom of the yard to visit the toilet or to fetch the coal. We now had an inside toilet although the cut up newspaper still hung on a nail inside the door, I often wondered later if toilet paper had been invented in those days.

The toilet was attached to the kitchen, something that would not be allowed by the planners nowadays, and we also had a bathroom. I have no memory of my first cleansing in a real bath. The facilities in Salisbury Street were the tin bath and boiling kettles of water on a Friday night. But we were now living in luxury and father, despite working 12 hours a day, was in seventh heaven with two gardens to care for. He soon became a skilled vegetable grower and indeed set up a small business breeding rabbits which he sold to neighbours to eke out the meat ration. It was often the job of my brother and I to feed the animals. That is possibly why to this day I cannot face rabbit in any

A certificate awarded to the author for coming second in a 'Bonny Baby' competition.

form. It brings back memories of seeing Dad kill them with a swift chop of the neck.

Garden City was a necessity, which had to come into being because of the terrible slum conditions in parts of the town, particularly on the Quayside. Blyth Borough Council, which was composed of a number of working men and business people, had decided it should be built. According to my father, heated discussions were held in the Council Chamber in Seaforth Street over the type of power to be installed.

One councillor, an employee of the Gas Board, was pushing for his company's product. There was stalemate until eventually a compromise was reached in that half the houses would have only gas and the others electricity. We, unfortunately, fell into the gas section of the Avenues which, apart from the additional cost of buying mantles for the lights, caused one big problem. When it came to listening to the radio, father had to buy accumulators in which the power was stored to run the radio. These portable batteries could be re-charged and an enterprising man called Gardner had set up a part-time business at his bungalow home in Newsham Road. He had electricity and had invested in a multiple charger. So it was that Frank and I had to take turns carrying the accumulator over Joe Percy's Bridge to where they were charged. As far as I recall it cost one penny a charge. I often wondered why my brother frequently offered to take my turn and it was only recently he confessed that Mr Gardner had the most beautiful daughter in Blyth who often served customers. He is only thirteen months older than me so I wonder why I failed to notice her. Each house with gas had three accumulators, which enabled one to be used while the other was being charged and the third held as an emergency. In this way we were able to listen to *ITMA* – It's That Man Again – starring Tommy Handley every week.

I don't know what happened to Mr Gardner or indeed his beautiful daughter. He possibly moved to the Bahamas with the money he cleaned up during the war for his home was less than 200 yards from the nearby gas-only Isabella Colliery and its hundreds of terraced houses. Incidentally the bridge got its name from being in close proximity to Joe Percy's general dealer's shop in Newsham Road. It actually spanned the Newsham to Blyth railway line along which trains from Newcastle and Ashington regularly ran.

The pedestrian approaches to Joe Percy's Bridge are still there but the structure and the line have long since disappeared. Instead we have a rather pleasant country-type walk from the railway crossing on Plessey Road to the Blyth Sports Centre.

Wartime meant every spare piece of land was being used for growing foodstuffs and the large field at the bottom of our back garden, on which Newlands School, now Ridley High was eventually built was no exception. It was planted with corn – a paradise for young lads and their secret dens while the older, more knowledgeable types, played doctors and nurses. I eventually graduated to this but it cost me a visit to see Charles Laughton in *Mutiny of the Bounty* after my younger brother, Bill, blabbed to my parents. I still remember the name of the 'nurse'.

Our enemies were the lads from Twenty-fifth Avenue and many a battle raged in the middle of the cornfield with chunks of soil being used as hand grenades.

The Anderson shelter, our protection during bombing raids, had already been installed in the back garden as far away from the house as possible and we fortunately did not have to use it too often. I can recall on one occasion hearing the noise of a plane and leaving the shelter just in time to see a German bomber flying low over the back field, I could clearly see the head of the pilot silhouetted against the searchlights.

While a land mine, a bomb on a parachute, landed on houses in Newsham not a mile away from our house killing some residents, I cannot recall the incident. Bombs were also dropped on Blyth Railway Station but again I must have been sound asleep as I cannot recall that incident either. What I can recall is seeing all the iron railings at my school, Princess Louise Infants and the adjoining Princess Louise Senior School, being removed to be used for the war effort. Later, when

Frank and Emily Harland, the parents of the author, on their golden wedding anniversary. Frank, who died at the age of 88, was the winding engineman at the Isabella Colliery while Emily is still going strong at 89 and managing an occasional visit to the Mecca Bingo Hall in the former Roxy Ballroom.

older, I learned there was not a scrap of iron or metal left in the town. I also remember being marched with my class to stand outside the Essoldo Cinema in Beaconsfield Street to cheer King George VI and Queen Elizabeth as they drove through the town.

Some time later in the war I was again marched to Beaconsfield Street this time to see the remains of a German aircraft being towed on a low loader. I often wonder if it was the aircraft Rudolph Hess, Hitler's deputy, used to fly to England to seek a peace meeting. He bailed out and the plane crashed in the Borders.

There were two occasions during the war, which caused both sadness and happiness in our home. The first was when my mother was told her brother Billy had been killed in action in Belgium and the second when she was told her brother Albie had been captured by the Germans on Crete and was a prisoner in Germany.

The weekly treat for my parents was a visit to the cinema on a Friday night. This Friday they went to the Central when during a newsreel on our troops abroad my mother was convinced she had spotted Billy in the back of an army truck. She told the manager who ran the newsreel again and indeed it was her brother filmed shortly before his death.

Life for youngsters in the later war years was exciting. The Anderson shelter became redundant but there were obvious signs that something was about to happen. We no longer went to the beach to watch submarines leaving and entering Blyth Harbour. Blyth was one of the major ports for the underwater craft and while it was not possible to

An early picture of Blyth beach. During the Second World War it was extensively mined to thwart any possible German invasion. The Nazis did not arrive but there were casualties. An army sergeant and a private were blown up by one of the mines and a third was seriously injured. It was also rumoured that the giant guns pointing seawards from the concrete emplacements, which are still on the dunes, were in actual fact painted telegraph poles!

get on the beach because of barbed wire fences, we were still able to use the promenade.

Plessey Checks, on the south side of Bedlington, became one of our favourite haunts for that was where the Yanks were. It was early 1944 and American soldiers were using the small cliff faces to practise with live ammunition, firing mortars and other such devices against the rock. If the red flag was flying at the bottom of Hartford Bank then the woods were temporarily out of bounds. If the green flag flew then you were free to enter. On this particular day I was the youngest of a group of seven and we arrived just in time to see the Americans raise the green flag.

Now to get to the woods you had to pass the cliffs, which were strewn with shell cases and the like, a haven for inquisitive youngsters. Naturally we rummaged among the debris and I uncovered what appeared to be a large cigarette lighter. It had a wire at one end and what appeared to be a thinner wire out the other. Ron Addison was the leader of our group and he immediately offered to swap me two shell cases for the 'lighter'. I refused and put it in my pocket. Little did I know that Ron, who was five years older, knew exactly what I had.

Our house in Twentieth Avenue had coal fires and as I sat in front of the living room blaze I took the 'lighter' from my pocket and endeavoured to burn off the piece of wire, which was preventing it standing upright, by holding it against the red coals. The full force of the resulting explosion, fortunately for me, was away from my body and made a very large dent in the large, heavy, black iron kettle standing on the hob. With blood oozing from my right hand I staggered into the kitchen and put it under the tap before passing out. I came round in the ambulance taking me to the Royal Victoria Hospital in Newcastle. My younger brother, Billy, found part of my thumb under the radio while the end of my forefinger was apparently hanging by a shred of skin. The official inquiry into the incident, as I spent two weeks in hospital, showed that Ron Addison had correctly identified the 'lighter' as an unexploded detonator.

I have to say the surgeons did a fine job repairing my hand in that I have never suffered any extreme sensitivity where the skin and nerves were sewn together. The only thing I cannot do is pick up a needle between what remains of my right hand thumb and forefinger. Eventually I went to the County Court at Morpeth where Judge Stephenson awarded me £500 damages against the United States government to be held in trust until I was twenty-one.

I can recall listening to the radio on June the 6th and hearing Alvar Liddell announce that the Allies had landed 'on the coast of Europe.' Even though I was nine it had little impact on our Twentieth Avenue gang and we continued to enjoy ourselves diving through the privet hedges at the front of the gardens which were so thick they catapulted you back on to your feet.

Life revolved around the cinema, playing in the street and school in that order. We had a large selection of cinemas with four in the centre of Blyth and one at Newsham. They were always vying for trade and the Essoldo hit on the gimmick of live entertainment at their Saturday morning children's show. A lady accordionist played a medley of songs but always started with the Essoldo song, which we all sang with gusto. It was an easy song to remember. It went:

E. S. S. O. L. D. O. … E. S. S. O. L. D. O. … E. S. S. O. L. D. O.
We go to the … EE … SOL … DOH.

By now I was attending Crofton Junior School where the headmaster was a strict disciplinarian called Mr Redford. He was a former naval officer and a keen yachtsman and could not abide boys putting their hands in their pockets. Morning assembly was where he warned us of the dire consequences if anyone transgressed. In an absent-minded moment I was caught standing in the hall with both hands hidden from view just as he passed. 'Boy,' he roared, 'to my office.' He administered three strokes of the cane to my left hand.

By now meals were being provided for some schools at a central hall at St Wilfrid's Roman Catholic School. For Crofton pupils it meant walking a mile to be fed. Although severe rationing was in effect, the dinner ladies managed to present us with well balanced meals even though we could have eaten them twice over. They certainly were not memorable as, for the life of me, I cannot remember one lunch menu. Brother Frank though says he hated them because they always contained tomatoes.

I can remember my brother and I after one lunch being caught by Mr Watson, the school board man, stealing apples from a garden at the top of Marine Terrace. The street, incidentally, was originally named Windsor Terrace but was renamed in protest at Edward Windsor abdicating.

It is strange how fate takes a hand. Mr Watson gave Frank and I a severe telling off but did not report us to Mr Redford. Some twenty-two years later I bought Mr Watson's house, not 100 yards from the scene of our apple 'crime', from his widow.

It was at Crofton Junior School I sat, and failed, my Eleven Plus. A year earlier my brother Frank had succeeded and joined the blazer, collar and tie brigade.

Blyth Grammar School in Plessey Road, which is now Delaval Middle, was the only higher learning establishment in the borough. Bright pupils were admitted, not just from Blyth, but also the surrounding areas reducing the number of places available to pupils of the town. So it was I found myself in the 'A' stream at Princess Louise Senior School. On reflection the teaching was appalling with little or no attempt at enthusing pupils. History lessons consisted on occasions of the teacher reading from '1066 And All That' while in our music lesson we were asked to put notes on blank manuscript paper to see if we had accidentally composed a tune. The arrival of a new headmaster, Ted Short saw some improvement. Mr Short, later to become Minister for Education and Deputy Prime Minister in a Labour Government, set about installing a house system. There were four houses named after animals. I was in Stag.

It was during an English lesson I wrote what was to be my first published work – a poem. Even now it is imprinted on my memory.

> Through the forest dark at night
> Glaring sharply, green and bright
> Peer through the foliage, two eyes,
> Even though the tiger tries to hide them from his enemies
> Who run away to taunt and tease
> At a distance far to great
> For the mighty tiger
> Who must wait once again to catch his prey.

I was asked if I had heard of a poem called 'Tiger, Tiger' as mine scanned almost exactly. I knew, as did my English teacher, there was as much chance of me knowing that poem as there was of his colleague burning his copy of '1066 And All That'.

As I also did not know what 'scanning' meant it was decreed that my poem should be printed and distributed to every pupil in the school. On the basis of this and the fact I had won an essay competition on Road Safety I was entered in the Thirteen Plus examination, which was a late entry to the Grammar School. Again I failed.

The 'A' stream I was in boasted some good and bad characters and it was because of the latter I learned that Ted Short, now Lord Glenmara, believed in corporal punishment. In those days we still had inkwells in our desks which were topped up each morning. A favourite game of the 'bad boys' was to dip paper in the ink and flick them by means of a ruler on to the ceiling. Soon after our classroom had been decorated, several ink splodges appeared on the ceiling. Mr Short duly

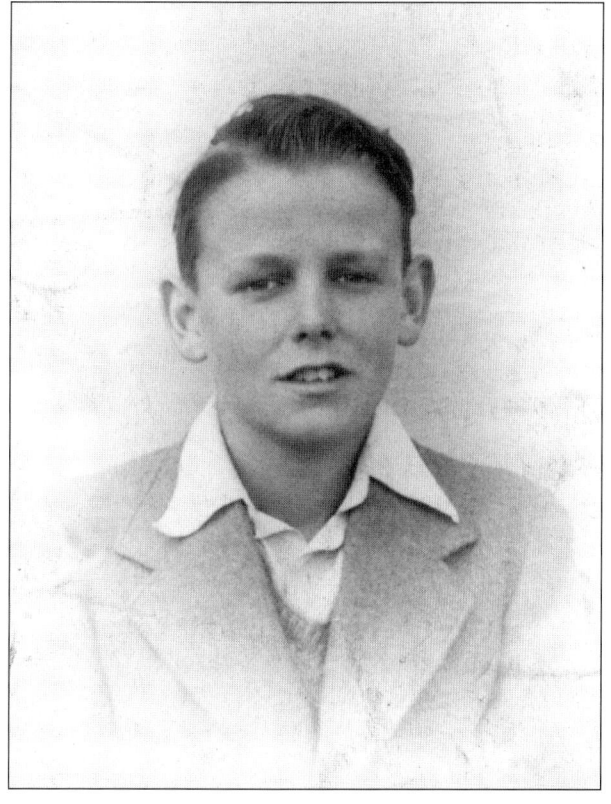

A young author wearing the customary open necked shirt when aged thirteen and attending Princess Louise Senior School where Ted Short, later to be deputy prime minister, was headmaster.

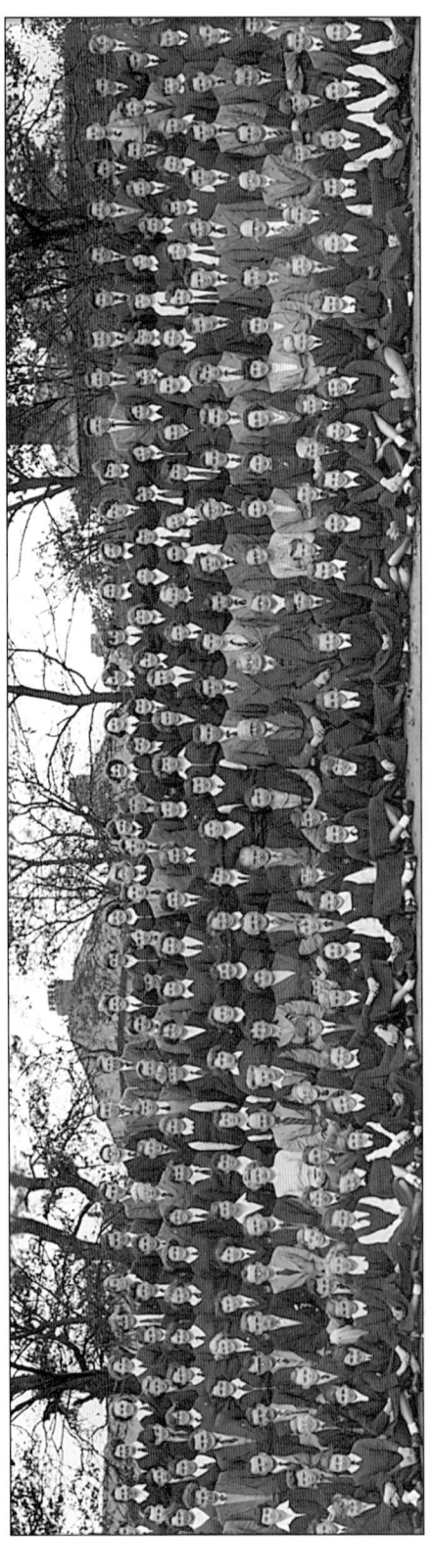

Blyth Grammar School, 1954. Back row: Unknown, unknown, unknown, unknown, unknown, unknown, Frank Scott, unknown, Alan Mackenzie, unknown, unknown, Ann Fletcher, unknown, unknown, unknown, unknown, unknown, Geoff Buglas, Bill Stephens, Peter Robertson, John Hogg, Ronnie Patterson, Colin Percy, George Pearson, Bill Thompson, David Ramsey, Melvin Moody (he turned out a number of times for Blyth Spartans). Second row from front: Pat Orange (Head Girl), Mr Tomlinson, Mr Hodgson, Harry Rowlands (became well-known local author, H.J. Rowlands), Dan Dolan, Jim Mackenzie, Frank De la Motte, Mrs Simpson, unknown, Harry Burnip, unknown, Mrs Burrell (school secretary), Major John George Hay, Alec Wilson. Miss Joyce (Headmistress, Girls), Mr Hanson (Headmaster), Percy Day (Deputy Headmaster), Miss Farrow, Phyllis Hough, Miss Cole, Lorna Chrisp, Miss Foggo, Mrs Swinney, Mrs Wilmina Dixon, Tom Hughes, Ron Phillipson, Mr Hunter, Tom Procter, Jack Hudspeth, Peter Hudson (Head Boy). Ray Smith, sitting in front of Miss Foggo, played for Blyth Spartans at the age of eighteen. Included in the third row from the front starting from immediately behind Miss Foggo: John Watts, Michael Jackson, unknown, Fred Stokoe, Guy Henderson (he became England Boys golf champion), Ken Christie, Bill Butler, unknown, Bill Caisley, unknown and Bob Shaw.

appeared and demanded to know the culprits. We knew the two who had done it but no-one was prepared to squeal. The future Deputy Prime Minister then gave us half an hour to think about it. On his return we again refused to say. At that all thirty-five of us were lined up in the passage alongside his office and each, in turn, was given three on each hand. My right hand, which was perfectly healed, was not excused.

In my final year, Ted Short appointed me head boy which was a very important job as I was called out of class at every opportunity to act as 'gofer' for him and other senior staff. Some education!

Came the time I was due for my interview with the Blyth Careers Officer at his office in Wellington House in the centre of town. 'And what do you want to be when you leave school?' he asked.

'A journalist,' I replied.

'I am afraid you have no chance.'

How wrong he was.

Dental Hygiene

Dental hygiene among the working classes was unheard of, as far as I can recall, in the 1940s. I cannot remember having a toothbrush until I invested in one from my earnings as an ice cream salesman, but more of that later. It was the custom and practice to have all your teeth removed as soon as they started causing continuous trouble and to have them replaced with a false set.

My parents, uncles and aunts all had false teeth and it was assumed the offspring would follow suit. Dental 'hygiene' in those days consisted of a trip to a mysterious and dreaded man who was the town tooth puller. My mother took me when I was about ten after I had suffered agony with one of my larger molars. He sat me in a household easy chair into which I sank deeply allowing my head to rest against the back. There was a wash basin but no running water and as my mother watched he gave me an injection. I dread to think about the condition of the needle, as there was certainly no sterilising unit. An injection and tooth pull cost more than just a pull, which, my mother hard up though she was, thankfully declined on my behalf. The time waiting for the injection to come into effect was the worst as I could see the pincers, which were to remove the offending tooth. Eventually the task was done and my mother counted out the sixpence fee, money she could ill afford. She wrapped a scarf around my face, 'to stop the cold getting into the hole,' she said and off we went home.

I often smile to myself when I see youngsters in Blyth nowadays with a scarf around their mouths indicating to one and all they have had a tooth extraction.

While one can criticise parents for being ignorant about the care of the mouth, it was a lesson I certainly learned as both my daughters have perfect teeth – and no extractions.

My mother in later life told me the tooth puller also operated a house call service and that he had pulled all her bottom teeth out – fourteen in all – while she sat in a chair in her front room in Maddison Street. And he was also prepared to operate in the kitchen of his own home as brother Frank discovered when he was taken there by my mother to have a tooth extracted.

Now to my career as an ice cream salesman. I was at college at the time and needed to make some extra cash. This is where Lovats Ice Cream manufacturers, of Newsham, Blyth, came in. In those days each town had their own ice cream makers. In Blyth it was the Seghini's and Lovats. A former schoolfriend tipped me off Lovats were looking for driver-salesmen. Not motor vehicles but horse drawn 'chariots'. I would be paid a basic seven shillings and sixpence for a twelve hour plus day but also commission on my sales. Mr Lovat knew what he should get back for a tub of ice cream.

The other drivers quickly taught me how to 'cream off the top', if you pardon the pun, by using less ice cream on cornets and wafers. In effect robbing the customers of their full amount. It was standard practice as the feeling was the commission was too low. I can remember bumping into my pal, who was still working for Lovats, when we were out on our rounds and having a chariot race along Renwick Road and over the railway crossing which led to Blyth Railway Station.

In those days I was a keen attender at the Roxy Ballroom on a Saturday afternoon because not only were we taught to dance but also it was an opportunity to get near the opposite sex. The Bradford Barn dance was the most popular among the lads as this gave you the opportunity to dance, albeit for a just minute and a bit, with every girl on the floor as you changed partners frequently.

One Saturday I was out early with my pony and trap on my ice cream round when I came across some of my Roxy friends. I decided there and then I was going to join them but what to do with the horse and cart? I decided to tie the horse up in the field behind our home in Twentieth Avenue, where Ridley High School now stands, and to put my ice cream container in the bath at home. I then removed the dry ice, which kept the container cool, from the cart and put that in the bath as well. My horse was in seventh heaven with as much grass as it could eat. I went off to the Roxy with my mother's condemnation ringing in my ears and thoroughly enjoyed myself for a couple of hours. I dashed back after the dance, removed the ice cream and dry ice from the bath and went out to achieve my sales target. The only problem was the dry ice had done its job too well and the ice cream was absolutely solid. I ended up having to chip the ice cream out to provide the cornets for the kids and my sales target went out the window. As did my job.

WE GROW BY INDUSTRY

Setting sail for North Blyth and periwinkling at the bottom of the North Pier sea wall was a terrific adventure for youngsters after the Second World War. The 'sea' voyage lasted only five minutes – depending on the tide – but it gave passengers the chance to see what boats were being dismantled at the Hughes Bolckow shipbreaking yard just north of the ferry landing. Alas this is also an industry which has died.

Whoever thought up the Borough of Blyth motto 'We Grow by Industry' certainly hit the nail on the head in those long ago years. Blyth was a hive of coalmining, shipbuilding and coal exporting. More than 1,000 men were employed by the Blyth Dry Docks and Shipbuilding Company whose land stretched almost the full length of Regent Street right up to the old chain ferry which ran from Blyth to North Blyth. In my youth it was the chain ferry skippered by 'Captain' Seaman Warnes which took us to the rocks outside the north pier where we clambered down the steel ladders set in the concrete wall of the pier to hunt for winkles. After they were boiled we could eat them with impunity although they did taste saltier when raw!

Mr Warnes got his honorary title from his long years at sea but his voyages in those days were being towed on two huge chains the 100 or so yards, depending on the tide, between the two concrete ferry ramps. The ferry itself could carry four cars which ran on to the centre of the vessel while cyclists and passengers used the two cabins on either side. When ships came into or left the River Blyth the chains were dropped to the river bed. The ferry was eventually withdrawn by Blyth Harbour Commission on the grounds of cost and although it was replaced by a passenger only vessel which detoured to drop and pick up workers at Cambois Power Station, the life of the residents of the terraced rows of North Blyth was considerably blighted.

When ideas were being sought for projects for the Millennium I suggested to Dave Stephens, the leader of Blyth Council, that a footbridge over the river from the end of Bridge Street to North Blyth, where the old Seven Stars pub was, be considered. It would, I said, open up and bring life to an almost dead area. Unfortunately, Mr

Regular users of the High Ferry were workers at Cambois Pit, Hughes Bolckow Shipbreaking Yard and residents of Cambois and North Blyth and later those employed at the Blyth Power Station at the head of the river. Cycles were essential for local residents, particularly those from Cambois, as bus services to the ferry on the North side were few and far between.

Stephens failed to be enamoured with the idea as he felt the new bridge at Bebside – a round trip of some seven miles from Blyth to North Blyth – was sufficient. Possibly an approach to Wansbeck Council, in whose area North Blyth is contained following the demise of Bedlingtonshire Urban Council, might have resulted in the idea falling on more fertile ground.

As a locally based journalist the launching of a new ship at Blyth was an occasion to celebrate and it was there in the company's offices deep inside the yard I had my first taste of champagne and canapés.

In those days after the Second World War workers brought sandwiches or headed home during the established lunch hour – noon until one o'clock. To view the shipyard gates at a couple of minutes to noon was to see hundreds of men on cycles ready for the off. When the gates opened spot on the hooter, which could be heard throughout the town alerting the wives their husbands were on their way, they poured out of the yard. The traffic gridlocks of today are nothing compared to the exodus. It was so dense it was impossible to cross Regent Street for several minutes as the workers pedalled furiously to their homes. The reason for speed was understandable. If they failed to get back by the second one o'clock hooter the gates were locked and they lost half a shift. On one occasion the timekeeper, a man called Billy Farley, locked out his brother George who arrived late!

The demise of Blyth shipyard began in the late 1950s as Japan, starting its post-war recovery, enlarged its building capacity and turned out ships faster and cheaper than British companies. (See page 24.)

It was coal which provided most of the jobs in the borough of Blyth with the Bates, Isabella, Bebside, Delaval and Crofton Mill pits flourishing inside and just outside the town. They were controlled under private enterprise from the Cowpen Colliery Offices, now turned into the Albion Court rest home opposite the Lidl store. Delaval was the first pit to go under and it was also the pit which boasted a fantastic waste heap. Over the years the unwanted residue from the pits was tipped alongside the colliery and internal combustion caused it to catch fire. The Delaval heap, when it burned out, left tremendous sculptures of red coke-like structures which towered above us as we lived out our childhood fantasies of what the moon was like. The heap was removed many years ago and is now part of the 18-hole Blyth Golf Course.

The Isabella heap was a different matter. It was still burning and children were given numerous warnings to avoid it as it was possible to sink into the inferno. It is still there overlooking part of the Newsham Farm Estate and the post-war houses which comparatively recently replaced the colliery rows. But the fires have long since gone and excellent landscaping has turned it into a rather nice country walk.

After a spell working in Cambridge I returned to Blyth and while awaiting a vacancy for my second spell on the *Blyth News – Ashington Post* I took a position as clerk to Jack Barrass, the manager of Crofton Mill Pit. This was in 1955 just a few years after nationalisation.

Jack, who lived at Seaton Sluice, was a kindly, good natured soul brought up in the privatised coal industry and not completely enamoured with the red tape of public ownership. He was particularly despairing of interference from the now established group, area and divisional levels of administration. One example was the introduction of Standard Costs Departments. They were set up to inform the manager of the costs of working certain faces in the pit. Clerks were sent to work at each pit to carry out the calculations but the only problem was Jack Barrass had the information from his overmen and deputies two days before it was produced by the costing clerks.

Even though the coal industry was nationalised there was still some private enterprise involved in mining with groups of miners – cavils as they were known – putting in bids to work certain areas underground. One group of lads had been complaining the coal face they were working, which was some five miles under the North Sea, was extremely damp and were seeking wet payment in addition to the agreed figure. To strengthen their case they marched into Jack's office at the end of a shift, threw a handful of crustaceans on his desk, and said, 'There, we told you it was wet – we've just holed into a shrimp bed.'

Jack looked up over his horn rimmed glasses, looked down at the red creatures, and retorted, 'You daft buggers – they're cooked.'

Just how bad and wasteful the nationalisation red tape was came home to me forcefully during my brief spell as manager's clerk. My duties included compiling a weekly report on the amount of explosives used underground. The weekly figures were then compiled as monthly, quarterly, half yearly and annual reports. I dutifully completed the reports and sent them off to the area office at the appropriate times. It was only when I started on the annual report I discovered I had inadvertently over-estimated the explosives by 364 thousand tonnes. It was an error included in the quarterly and half year reports and had not been spotted further up the chain – a clear indication the National

The author's father, Frank Harland, was the man who lowered the miners down the Isabella Pit into the bowels of the earth from the winding house which can just be seen to the left of the fuel storage tanks next to the pit sign. When Isabella closed only the Bates and Crofton Mill pits remained in the town. The smouldering pit heap referred to in the above article was south of the buildings.

Coal Board had been turned into an inefficient bureaucracy of filing clerks.

In those days ponies were still being used in the local pits and one of the highlights of the year was the start of the two weeks pit holidays when the animals, which were kept underground fifty weeks of the year, came to the surface for their annual break. They were turned out in fields lying between the Isabella and Bates pits and it was a truly amazing sight to see them frolicking at the freedom of it all.

Crofton Mill was one of the last Blyth pits to use ponies and there were so many underground we had a surface horse keeper whose job it was to make sure the horse-manure brought by tubs to the surface was put in the right place, i.e. well away from the pit head, canteen and offices. The only way he apparently could stick the job and its odours was by drinking copious amounts of Newcastle Brown Ale and so it was not unknown for him to be sometimes the worse for wear when he finished his shift. Being a non-car owner his transport as befits a professional horse keeper, was a pony and trap and many a night his clever animal took him and his drunken stupor, home. Some of the younger apprentices at the pit decided to play a prank on him. One night as he slumped on the driving seat the group led the pony to a five barred gate, unhitched the animal, pushed the shafts through the gate, and rehitched the pony. To the day he died he was still trying to figure out how it happened.

Having only once travelled underground at the pit, courtesy of the under-manager Sammy Mullen who made sure I crawled the wettest and smallest face, I can say I do not mourn the passing of the coal industry. I mourn the passing of the tremendous camaraderie in the most dangerous of occupations, the loss of full employment from which Blyth has not yet fully recovered and the sense of family belonging. While men were not born to work in the bowels of the earth it was their efforts which earned Blyth the title of the biggest coal exporting port in Europe. It was a title Donald Kent, the general manager of Blyth Harbour Commission, was extremely proud of and any hint of criticism in print of the port and commission led to journalists being summoned to his office near the Quayside for a dressing down. Although the fault might lay at head office with bad subbing or a poor headline it was the man on the spot – usually me – who faced the music.

The loss of industry in the town also meant the loss of a vibrant and alive community. Shipping brought in seamen and seamen brought in the women of the night mainly to be found in the Commercial pub which stood on the site now occupied by the entrance to the Keel Row Shopping Mall. Full employment meant money and time for leisure. The Commercial was just one of several pubs which ringed the Market Place, the Globe being another venue this one being popular with the white collar brigade – teachers, journalists, etc.

I happened to be working in Blyth in the years industry declined and I wrote a number of stories about how it was turning into a dormitory town and regrettably I was not wrong.

The Closure of Blyth Shipyard

On Wednesday, 1st March 1967 the Journal newspaper carried an article – ghosted by your author – by Harry Mitcheson, who, over 40 years, rose from office boy to become the last general manager of Blyth Dry Docks and Shipbuilding Company, in which he told the full story of the collapse of Blyth Shipyard. It is reproduced here in full.

'The first hint I had was a phone call from our London office asking me to break my holiday and meet a Mr Wilson at the yard the following day. After visiting an exhibition in Newcastle in the morning, I headed for the yard. The day was 3rd August 1966.

'In my office were three men and a woman. I recognised one as Mr James Wilson who had visited the yard earlier in the year when we were discussing the possibility of installing a new dry dock.

'I knew him as a man in charge of a department of a London firm dealing with the formation and winding up of companies. Now, he told me, he was here as a receiver. I cannot recall any emotional reaction to the news that the company was to be wound up. He was the new boss and I had a job to do to help him all I could.

'When I did have time to think, I realised the shock the news would be to the men who were on holiday at the time, so we decided to call a Press Conference. On reflection I did not feel any resentment at all to Mr Wilson's presence. It was his job to get £800,000 out of the yard for the bank and during the succeeding months I found him quite a pleasant fellow to work with.

'I have been at a bit of a loss to understand the reason why the bank took the action it did. We have carried an overdraft of £750,000 for many years. It is not something one worries about because it is working capital you have to have.

'The overall debts of the yard, at the time the receiver moved in, were in the region of £2,500,000, but, in normal times, the plant, land and buildings would cover it. In addition you have money to come in from the building of ships and from repair customers.

'To analyse the events leading up to the closure one has to go back to the end of the golden years – from the beginning of the war up to about 1961. Things then began to get tough because of the shipping slump and increased competition from abroad.

'Shipbuilders, generally and we were no exception, wanted to retain their skilled men and adopted a policy of going after orders with tenders that were not lucrative. Everyone expected to weather the storm. This policy, as far as we were concerned, landed us in trouble. The starting point was when we decided to try to move into the dredger building market.

'We were forced to do it because of the changing times and to keep our men employed. We obtained an order for a dredger to be named the *Tideway*. Our lack of experience in this field caused us to be six months late in delivery and also pushed the costs up. To get it off the stocks as quickly as we could; we stopped looking for repair work and halted our plans for diversification. We never really recovered from this.

'One diversification which proved profitable was the industrialised housing section. We were busy on a contract for 98 dwellings at Newburn and had an order from Blyth for 102.

'To expand even further we built a factory at the Kitty Brewster Industrial Estate. This had just been completed when the receiver moved in. Even on our initial orders we made a profit. It is still something which could go if someone was prepared to take over the factory.

'Generally speaking, the industrial relations at the Blyth yard were good. During my time there I can only remember one strike and that was during the General Strike.

'The industrial troubles we did have stemmed from the Tyne yards. District meetings of the men would mean the trouble being brought to Blyth. Our men did follow the Tyne. The demands were no more than were being sought at other yards but, again speaking generally, the demands were excessive. Wage demands went up by anything up to 20 per cent and this is a lot to stand on any order.

'I don't really blame the men. It is natural that if you are getting £20 on the Tyne for a certain job and £18 at Blyth you should try to get £20. The size of the yard or the orders did not enter into it.

'We were on the point of getting over all the demarcation troubles when the receiver stepped in. We had a scheme which had been more or less accepted by the men. The men were prepared to accept the sharing of benefits. Whatever savings there were on a ship, the men, office staff and company would get a percentage.

'We had a contract for a 23,000-ton bulk carrier on which work was to have started in August. The engines had been ordered and we were preparing to order the steel when Mr Wilson arrived. That could have been the beginning of a big change at Blyth.

'Twelve months' grace and this is not just wishful thinking, and we could have been on the way up again.

'There has been speculation, since the closure, of the part Eric B.

Harry Mitcheson, having worked his way up from the bottom of the ladder, was a popular leader at Blyth Shipyard and its closure affected him deeply. That was very apparent to your author during the interview at his detached home in Horton Road, near Bedlington.

Moller and his brother, Ralph B. Moller, played in the collapse. Although they are not named as directors of the company, they ran the yard because Moller Trusts, based in Hong Kong, owned the Blyth Dry Docks and Shipbuilding Company.

'I firmly believe that they were not aware of the action contemplated by the bank. Had they been, there are things they could have done at Blyth which would have personally benefited them.

'Mention has also been made about the company being based in Hong Kong. When the Mollers took over the Blyth yard after the war, they had extensive Far East shipping interests including the Wham Poa shipyard in Hong Kong. The tax position may have come into it but it is also not unreasonable for businessmen to want to centralise their operations. All directors meetings of the Blyth company took place in Hong Kong.

'I believe that the reason for the bank foreclosure was the general decline in the shipbuilding industry. Personally I would not touch shipbuilding with a barge pole at present.

'Whatever happens, we have not lost as much money as other people. Once Mr Wilson gets his money from the yard, the liquidators will move in to get the money for the unsecured creditors. The shipyard will be badly missed by the town and for this reason I would like to see someone buy the place.'

Unfortunately, for the town and the unemployed, no one did come forward to take over the yard. Several concerns now occupy the site with a total workforce far, far smaller than in the shipbuilding days.

SECTION THREE

THE ROYAL, THE ROXY AND CINEMAS

The fifty-five ladies and gentlemen of the chorus in the 1961 production of White Horse Inn by the Blyth Operatic Society at the old Theatre Royal. Every seat was sold for the six performances of the show.

The only limited national fame the Theatre Royal in Trotter Street, Blyth, achieved was through the success of the Laurel and Hardy film partnership for the father of Stan Laurel managed it in the early part of the 20th century. And also, briefly in the 1960s, when a rather plump lady set the record for non-stop piano playing.

Further reflected glory came through television when it transpired the late Stratford Johns, who rose to fame through *Z Cars* and *Softy Softly*, was a member of a repertory company based at the Theatre Royal in the 1950s. Jim Bell, a former town councillor, and his wife, Leonora Rogers who ran a dancing school in the town, had Stratford, who was known in those days as Alan Johns, as a lodger for some time and Jim dined out for years on how his guest only had three black socks and washed one a night. Jim's friendship with the actor lasted long after he had gone on to television fame and he often visited him at his home in the London area.

Many of older generation of Blyth bemoan the fact the Theatre Royal was not saved from demolition. But in the 1960s the future of the theatre did not come high on the list of priorities of those in power.

The Vagabond King produced by the Blyth Operatic Society in 1965 was the last show staged at the Theatre Royal in Trotter Street before its demolition. Tom Easton is the man on the floor; Jimmy Russell is looking down at him; David Haxon, now a successful businessman in Alicante, Spain, is the soldier and the author is about to be arrested. It is easy to tell the picture was taken during the dress rehearsal as quite a lot of the ladies in the chorus are wearing their glasses!

Inside the Theatre Royal.

Indeed it would have cost many, many, thousands of pounds to have put it right. For a start it needed re-roofing. An example of this need was amply illustrated during the Saturday matinee performance of *Bless the Bride* by Blyth Amateur Operatic Society. The town's leading comedian, Jimmy Russell, was sat at a table in the middle of the stage and was due to get drunk in a short space of time on red wine. The wine was indeed strawberry coloured water, much to his regret. But Jim's glass was placed in such a position that rainwater dropped through a hole in the roof exactly into the glass and with such a force it could be seen by the audience. It was a natural for Jim who had the place in an uproar with his antics in following the drops from the roof into his glass!

Another example of the need for cash being spent on the building was the late Tom Easton, a well respected teacher at Newlands School, later Ridley High, but also an amateur thespian of some note. As a former navy man, he gallantly volunteered to wear waterproofs to wade thigh deep through the regular floods in the boiler room, complete with aquatic rats, to stoke the coal fire which heated the theatre and, not, I hasten to add, the dressing rooms which boasted only cold water. The gallery at the theatre was deemed to be dangerous which meant only the stalls and circle were available to the public. Even then it was an impressive place and almost acoustically perfect. My one regret is that I did not see it at its finest.

With the advent of television and the demise of variety and other live entertainments the Theatre Royal fared badly. Two professional repertory companies tried to keep the place alive but many is the time my wife and I sat in the circle on our regular Friday theatre night freezing along with less than a dozen hardy souls.

Little did we know then, huddled in our overcoats, that we were watching a young actor who was to become a household institution in the North East – a certain Mr Mike Neville. Mike appeared in several plays at the Theatre Royal in 1958 for the Royal Repertory Players – a fact which has come to light through the diligence of Trevor Harder, the director of the Beaconsfield Operatic Society. Trevor is a theatre buff and indeed boasts some artefacts at his home in Blyth which he rescued when the Theatre Royal was being demolished. He also obtained copies of programmes bearing Mike's name.

Trevor sent a photocopy of one to Mike at the BBC studios in Newcastle and got a thank you letter in return which revealed that the 'Pamela Edwards' in the cast of the play later became his wife. 'We met at the Theatre Royal,' Mike wrote.

Films were introduced but they also failed and the owner, Sol Sheckman, of Essoldo fame closed it in 1965 and the site is now part of the Keel Row shopping mall car park.

The Essoldo chain of cinemas was famous throughout the North East but many were puzzled as how the name of the chain was arrived at. Actually it was composed by using the initial letters of Sol, his wife Esther and daughter, Dorothy.

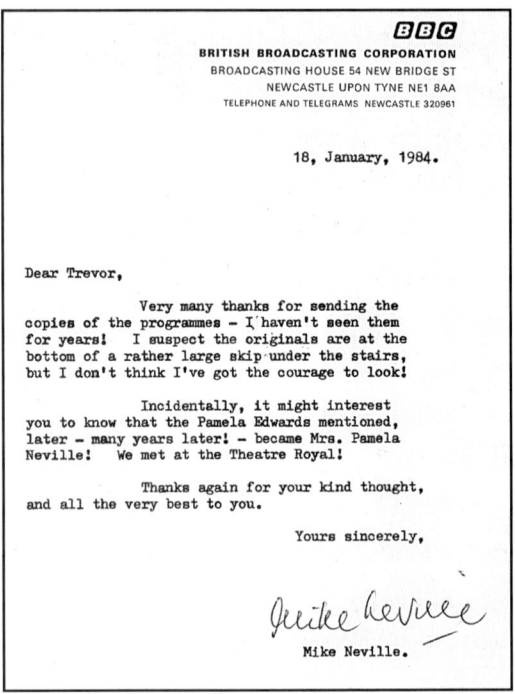

Because of the lack of public support during the Rep season at the Theatre Royal in Blyth not many people knew that Mike Neville had appeared there in 1958 and indeed met his wife, Pam, while playing in The Manic. Trevor Harder, a leading Blyth theatre buff, rescued some programmes when the theatre was being demolished and sent a copy off to Mike at the BBC in Newcastle. He received this very nice letter in reply.

Another chain in the area was the Wallaw group with cinemas in Blyth, Bedlington Station, Newbiggin and Ashington. This name was derived from the owner Walter Lawson – again the initial letters. Only the Wallaw in Blyth survives. But the finest cinema in the town was undoubtedly the Essoldo with a capacity of around 1,600, beating the Wallaw by almost 200. This stood on a site in Beaconsfield Street, which is now occupied by the Central Methodist Church, and actually backed on to the old Hedley Young's store now Poundstretchers. Its upstairs circle foyer was so huge a dance could have been held there if it were not for the thick, pile carpets.

Above: This view of Beaconsfield Street from what is now the bus station shows the Hedley Young's store but there is no sign yet of the Essoldo cinema which is to be built on the site of the last block of the store – the three storied section being approached by the horse and trap. To the left, surrounded by iron railings, is the Thomas Knight Memorial Hospital.

The Central Cinema, drinking fountain, telephone and police boxes have long since gone from Blyth Market Place. But the North side is virtually the same with no new building having taken place although the trades in the various shops have changed considerably.

The Central Cinema in Blyth Market Place was the oldest in the town and boasted extremely popular courting seats. These were a couch seat without a centre arm rest and were situated, where else, in the back row of the stalls and the circle. The building was multi-purpose for the structure incorporated Martins Bank on the Waterloo Road side and Baird's the butchers on the side facing Woolworth's. Ironically enough, the courting seats are now back in favour with some new multiples installing them. The Central Cinema backed on to the Zion Methodist Church in Waterloo Road but both, alas, went the way of the demolition men in the later post-war years.

There was another cinema out of the town centre and this was the small one storied Plaza at Newsham. The building still exists on Newcastle Road and is nowadays in use as a church but in my childhood it was known as the cinema where you could see Flash Gordon and other classic serials on a Saturday afternoon. It was essential to get a seat towards the back of the steeply raked auditorium and that is why there were always long queues. The reason quickly became obvious if you were late and had to be seated in the front section.

If you were in the best seats and needed to use the cinema toilet you lost your seat to someone from the front so nobody moved and instead did what they had to do as they sat. The torrent of waste water meant those in the front three rows had to keep their feet up. This did not happen at the brand new Roxy Cinema which was built after the war on the site of the old Hippodrome Cinema which was alongside the Roxy Ballroom in the central bus station area of the town. I cannot recall any clear memories of the Hippodrome although I have a fancy when I was about three my brother and I got in on a Saturday afternoon for a jam jar each. Recycling is certainly not new for in those days manufacturers paid for the return of jars and bottles. Indeed long after the Second World War, pop bottles were a source of income to cash minded youngsters.

The Roxy Cinema was single-storied but I am afraid it did not last long as it fell victim to the fall off in cinema attendances brought about by the television boom. It became a Bingo hall and was eventually extended to take in the Roxy Ballroom. On the few occasions I have been into the main hall I almost weep to see tables and chairs screwed into what was once the finest sprung dance floor in Northumberland.

The Roxy Ballroom was tremendously popular particularly for teenagers on a Saturday afternoon. It was there you not only met the girls but were also taught how to dance properly. Tuition was given by a ballroom dancer called George Pitkeathley and his wife and partner Betty who took us through all forms of dance. Even now I can still perform Latin American, Old Time and Modern but am a bit rusty on American square dancing. From the Saturday afternoon sessions you graduated to the evening sessions with Modern dancing on a Monday and Saturday, Old Time on a Tuesday, private functions on Wednesday, Barn, Scottish and American square dancing on Thursday and a mixed programme on Friday.

The private Wednesday night dances at the Roxy Ballroom were a popular post-war feature in the town enabling the men and women to get dolled up in all their finery. This picture, taken in the 1950s, is believed to be the Post Office annual ball. The dances were staged to a strict format with a whist drive being held on the balcony of the Roxy from about seven o'clock followed by the dance about an hour and a half later.

Tommy Bell and his ten-piece orchestra provided music at the Roxy for many years. Tommy was regarded as the 'Mr Music' of the town and his musicians were always impeccably dressed in evening suits and bow ties. Tommy, an excellent accordionist, was a bit of a character who, on occasions, after liberally indulging in the drink was not beyond halting a dance in mid-stream to berate the dancers for not doing it properly. He also took a delight in encouraging local singers by letting them perform with his band. Frankie Riley, who became known as Blyth's answer to Frank Sinatra and who could quite easily have forsaken his profession as a cobbler to turn professional, was a regular as was Stan Beckwith, a rich baritone, Jim Bell and indeed I sang my first song in public there.

The Wednesday night private functions were extremely popular and tickets were hard to come by. Among the organisations, which held annual black tie affairs, there were the Quaysiders, Blyth Shipyard, Hedley Young's, the Police and the Chamber of Trade. The annual Valentine Ball was also a tremendous draw.

Some of the private dances incorporated whist drives on the balcony which surrounded the dance floor on two sides. The whist started at seven o'clock and the dance at half past eight. Press Balls were also staged there by the East Northumberland branch of the National Union

The famous bandleader, Ken Mackintosh, at the Roxy Ballroom chats to Tommy Bell, 8th February 1960.

The famous midweek dances at the Roxy Ballroom meant you got togged up in your best. Ray Dunn, the Blyth News photographer, took this picture on the balcony of the ballroom and, from left to right, are: Joan and Norman Waddle, Marian and Brian Lambert and Joan Dunn whose hand is being held by the author – with her husband's approval, of course.

of Journalists and always proved popular because of the number of prizes which could be won after being donated by local and national companies. One of the leading organisers was the NUJ chairman Johnny Brownlee who was employed by Kemsley and later Thomson newspapers as their Blyth district senior reporter. Top prize at one ball was a week for two at a Butlins holiday camp – a smashing prize in those days when cheap holidays abroad were unheard of. There were almost 200 prizes on the stall and before the doors were opened staff at

The programme for the 1964 press ball at the Roxy.

the Roxy asked if they could try their luck and it was agreed by the Press Ball committee they could. A bad decision it turned out to be for the first one purchased out of the thousands in the drum won the Butlins holiday! The barman, Les Armstrong, who took the prize and everyone who knew it had been claimed was sworn to silence while the punters tried their luck. Well, it was for charity!

The Roxy management also introduced cabaret spots. One well known star who appeared being the American singer Gene Vincent of *Be Bop a Lula* fame. Big bands were also brought in including Ken Mackintosh and his Orchestra and the musicians of the Nat Gonnela and Roy Fox outfits also being featured.

As with films, dance halls were hit by the changing entertainment values caused by the advent of television. Despite several attempts to get youngsters interested, dancing disappeared from the town as did the Roxy as a dance hall.

All smiles from Roxy Ballroom barman Les Armstrong after winning first prize - a week's holiday for two at Butlins - at the 1964 Press Ball. While Eileen Ritson and Rosemary Harland, wives of two of the organisers, smiled graciously at the presentation, the top prize was actually won before the doors were open to the public. Les had to keep quiet about his win until after the dance so as not to affect sales at the tombola stall!

SECTION FOUR

OPERATIC SOCIETIES

The first production of Calamity Jane in Blyth was staged at the Wallaw in 1971. Seen here is the author (Wild Bill Hickock) with Colin Brown, now a retired bank manager, as the bartender.

Two operatic societies exist in Blyth – the Blyth Operatic Society and the Beaconsfield, Blyth, Operatic Society. The Phoenix Theatre performs musicals but also produces straight drama.

At the outbreak of the Second World War, the Blyth Society closed down while Beaconsfield had already stopped performing in 1935. It was to take until 1959 for one of the societies to start up again. This came about through the efforts of a policewoman, Inspector Marjorie Garrett who was based in Blyth. Marjorie ran a ballet school in her spare time in a converted terrace house in Bridge Street where the Arriva bus garage now stands. She placed an advert in the *Blyth News* asking for parties interested in re-starting the Blyth Society to turn up at the school for an exploratory meeting. The turn out, which included several pre-war members of the Society, was such that a committee was formed immediately. I was appointed secretary with Ted Hogg becoming chairman. Brian Lambert accepted the accompanists post and Albert Lawton took the conductor's baton. Marjorie took on the mantle of producer and it was subsequently agreed that *Maid of the Mountains* should be performed at Newlands School now Ridley High, the following March.

It was a desperate struggle to get enough men to join – a situation, which exists even today – and with two weeks to go until the production tenors and basses were still being accepted. By then Marjorie had relinquished the position of producer to become ballet mistress, with Councillor Mrs Renee Gallon taking over. I had to resign

Only four of this bevy of lovely ladies had ever appeared in a musical before – in the pre-war shows of Blyth Operatic Society. For the rest their debuts in The Maid of the Mountains at Newlands School in 1960 marked the beginning of the resurgence of amateur operatics in the town.

The first production by Blyth Operatic Society was Maid of the Mountains at Newlands School in 1960. Pictured shortly before the off are: Gerry Evans (Mayor of Santo), holding the mirror, John Courtney (Crumpet) and the author (General Malona).

as secretary because of work commitments and Ernie Clark stepped into the breach. It was a rousing success with every seat taken during the week's run despite the costumes being lost on their way to Blyth. Fortunately they arrived on the day of the dress rehearsal. Allan Powell, later to become quite well known on North East television and who still appears on BBC's *Look North* was at that time working for the *Blyth News* and played the part of the non-singing hero Baldasarre. The success of the show led to a decision to stage the second production at the larger Theatre Royal in Trotter Street in the centre of the town which had lain unused for two years.

It took an army of volunteers from the Society weeks to clean the place from top to bottom. The presence of a rat in the downstairs bar area, however, led to this being a 'men only' workplace. White Horse Inn proved to be another outstanding success with 'House Full' boards yet again going up from the first night. The show was to lead to a five year association of the Society with the theatre until it yet again closed its doors, this time for good.

The New Moon, which was the production in 1962, is memorable for

Jimmy Russell, Gerald Kelly and the author all dressed up and nowhere to sail as The New Moon had not yet arrived at the Theatre Royal in 1962. The dress rehearsal for the show lasted until after one o'clock in the morning and the first night audience was still in their seats until well after eleven o'clock. Fortunately the show was tightened up for the rest of the week. The cost nowadays of costuming The New Moon would be horrendous for any amateur operatic society. In 1963 the hire of costumes was much cheaper which is why these 50-odd members of the Blyth Society could look so elegant in the ballroom scene.

Six of the chorus girls from the production of The New Moon at the Theatre Royal in 1962. Back row: Bette Arkley and Rosemary Brown. Centre: Dorothy Dixon and Kathleen Duffell. Front: Nancy Martin and Ann Rix.

the fact the dress rehearsal dragged on until one in the morning, with most of the cast having to go to work in the morning, and the first night curtain did not come down until after eleven o'clock. It also nearly led to the roof over the stage being blown off! Part of the action involved a galleon coming alongside *The New Moon* which was in itself a ship. Loud explosions indicating a gun battle between the two vessels preceded this. The bangs were to be brought about by setting off charges in three metal bins at the back of the stage out of sight of the audience. At the dress rehearsal the bins were primed but a stagehand, a volunteer, put the lids, which were very definitely not to be used, securely back on the brand new bins. When the charges went off the lids flew 60 foot up in the air to jam in the roof while the bins splattered outwards as in a Tom and Jerry cartoon. Needless to say the stagehand was not allowed anywhere near the bins for the rest of the week.

The year 1963 saw *The Desert Song* returning to the Theatre Royal stage for the first time since 1934 and again it was a tremendous success. Dicky Davison, one of the tenors, is remembered fondly by other men in the cast for a particular incident during the show. The cue, 'We turn to Mecca and pray,' had the chorus of Riffs, turning their backs on the audience and kneeling. The subsequent singing of the prayer by his colleagues collapsed amid giggling and laughter after Dicky, bending down, very audibly broke wind.

Gerald Kelly, headmaster of Delaval Middle School and a magistrate, played the role of General Birabeau the father of the foppish Pierre who in reality was the Red Shadow, the leader of the Riffs. Gerald had been a member of the pre-war Society and in one show in the early 1930s did a standing jump backwards on to a kitchen table. It was a feat he

The Royal Northumberland Yacht Club headquarters in the South Harbour at Blyth was used for publicity photographs for the Blyth Operatic Society production of The New Moon in 1962. Taking the sea breeze is the author who played Captain Duval and Gerald Kelly who was the evil Vicomte Ribaud.

repeated as a party trick in the early years of the re-formed Society.

Gerald, though, became forgetful during one performance of *The New Moon*. He was playing the evil French spy called upon to interrupt a scene when the hero was being interrogated on the deck of the ship. Ted Hogg was the hero, I was the interrogator and my assistant was John Ritson, a fellow reporter with the *Blyth News* who was later to become news editor of the *Evening Chronicle*. When Gerald did not appear a series of ad-libs sailed forth to keep the action going, still without any effect. Eventually I sent John off to find the absentee. He returned shortly to whisper in my ear, 'Gerald says he's got the wrong costume on so can you miss out this part.'

It was during rehearsals for this show the well known bandleader, Ken Mackintosh, appeared with his orchestra at the Roxy Ballroom. He was prevailed upon to attend one of the rehearsals and indeed to wield the baton.

By this time moves were afoot for the re-formation of Beaconsfield Operatic Society. It had started life in 1924 as an offshoot of the Beaconsfield Street Methodist Church with performances in the church hall but lasted only until 1935 when *The Mikado* proved to be the last pre-war production. Alan Harder and Johnny Johnson were two of the Gilbert & Sullivan aficionados who helped re-start the Society with, appropriately enough, a performance of *The Mikado* on the Newlands

The social committee of Blyth Operatic Society is extremely active and one of the highlights is the New Year dance, which used to be held in the BRSA Social Club, known locally as 'The Bandroom'. Unfortunately it is now closed and the dances are held at the Seaton Sluice Social Club. Here at the Bandroom in 1973 are, from left to right: Marion Lambert, Margaret Davidson, Rosemary Harland, Catherine Wilkinson and Joy Jones. The all played Quakers Girls in the 1972 show.

School stage. Howard Davison, the brother of Dicky the windy tenor, was the musical director and Renee Gallon produced. Five more G&S productions followed until 1969 when the Society moved to the Wallaw for a performance of The Merry Widow. The Society has subsequently mixed modern musicals with a smattering of G&S. In recent years, thanks to a driving force called Trevor Harder, the Society's director and son of Alan, the public of East Northumberland has been able to see the North East premieres of new shows: *Hunchback of Notre Dame*, *Sweeney Todd* and, in 2002, *All4One*.

The Blyth Society, in the early days of its reformation, almost purchased its own hall. Negotiations for the single storied St John Hall in Goschen Street, which was used to train members of the ambulance organisation, were almost at the contract stage but the Society pulled out on the advice of their president and honorary solicitor John Knott. The deeds to the property could not be found. Subsequently the Blyth Society has used various venues for rehearsals and is now, as is the

South Pacific at The People's Theatre, Newcastle, became known as the musical with the moving palm trees. The trees can be seen in this photograph of the finale to the show with the author about to be re-united with Nellie Forbush (Hazel Thompson). The two trees were on trucks which enabled them to be moved about the stage during scene changes. Unfortunately for Jack Dixon, who was playing Lt Cable, they were moved behind him as he was singing Younger than Springtime to the dusky Polynesian maiden Liat (Jean Mellon) – not once but twice to the great hilarity of the audience and the bewilderment of Jack. Unfortunately the critics were in that night and that is why it is now known as 'the moving palm trees show'.

The famous bandleader Ken Mackintosh took time out during a performance by his orchestra at the Roxy Ballroom to conduct the Blyth Operatic Chorus during a rehearsal held in the Waterloo Hotel in 1964.

Alf Douglas as Luther Billis struts his stuff in South Pacific the 1971 production of the Blyth Operatic Society at the Wallaw Cinema. Helping him out are members of the male chorus including Jim Bell and John Browell.

Taking a breather during rehearsals for South Pacific at the Wallaw in 1971 are Blyth Operatic members. Kneeling: Una Ord and Joan Lockyer. Standing: Rosemary Harland, Brenda Wilkes, Marion Lambert, Brenda Johnson (on top of the mask), Elizabeth Dunn and Bette Arkley.

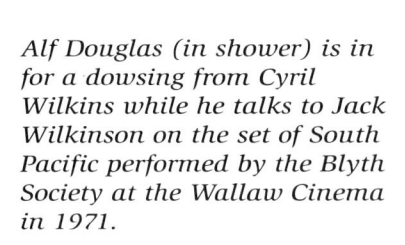

Alf Douglas (in shower) is in for a dowsing from Cyril Wilkins while he talks to Jack Wilkinson on the set of South Pacific performed by the Blyth Society at the Wallaw Cinema in 1971.

Beaconsfield Society, settled at the Spartan Hotel in Sixth Avenue. This has been made possible by the wholehearted support of the licensees, Pauline and Geoff Gainford, for on occasions their main function room is being used five nights a week for rehearsals.

The Desert Song was the Blyth Society's third production at the Theatre Royal in 1963 followed the next year by *Bless the Bride*. Sadly, *The Vagabond King* in 1965 proved to be the death knell of the fine old theatre. And it almost proved the death of the leading man, Francois Villon, played by me. At the dress rehearsal where I was about to be hung on a scaffold, six feet high, with a real, noosed rope around my neck, I saw that the executioner, played by chorus member Brian Cook, had fastened his end of the rope for convenience sake to the wooden rail alongside me. He quickly untied it following my unscripted outburst in which I pointed out what a trip or collapse could have done to my neck.

The after show party that year was tinged with sadness at the loss of the Theatre Royal but already a contingency plan had been made and the 1966 production of *Rose Marie* was staged at the Wallaw Cinema. How shows with a chorus of over 60 singers and dancers were put on in those days in a purpose-built cinema was a miracle. The Society had only a twelve feet depth of stage to work on and there was no fly tower which meant scenery could not be pulled up into the flies and had to

Bless the Bride was the 1964 production by the Blyth society in the Theatre Royal. Note the depth and width of the stage – a far cry from the rather cramped conditions prevailing at the Wallaw which was, of course, built as a cinema.

One of the perks of being a leading man is you get your picture taken with some of the beautiful dancing girls. Here the author, dressed for the part of General Estaban in Rio Rita at the Wallaw Theatre in 1969, is in the company of (left to right) Lesley Kennedy, Una Ord, Joan Lockyer, Brenda Wilkes and Barbara Lawton.

Despite regular appeals for the stage for the shy men of Blyth to join the ranks the Blyth Operatic Society continued to perform successfully on the Wallaw stage. This is the chorus of the 1969 production of Rio Rita.

be stored in the already congested wings. In addition the huge cinema screen had to be dismantled after the last film performance on the Saturday night before the dress rehearsal could be staged. This was a specialist job and a team of workmen was busy until the early morning at a cost of several hundred pounds to the Society. Dressing rooms in the stage area consisted of what was known as the 'Crush Room', in effect the old stalls waiting room, and the boiler room.

Blyth undoubtedly had the fittest chorus in the whole of the North East. For while the principals and young dancers had the accommodation near the stage the ladies of the chorus had to sprint from the stage, out into the back lane exposed to the elements, along the full length of the building, enter the rear exit and climb three flights of stairs to a large, well-lit and warmed room.

After the first year the committee decided a covered walkway made of scaffolding and tarpaulin had to be run alongside the building and eventually two portacabins were installed in the back lane. It was a

Wild Bill Hickock (the author) just does not believe what Calamity Jane (Doreen King) is telling him about how she saved the stage coach from numerous Indians. The musical was staged in the Wallaw Cinema in March 1971, watched by an audience of 7,500. Six months later the society produced South Pacific at the Wallaw. As it was regarded as something of a gamble it was initially going to be staged at Newlands School but the demand for tickets was such that it was switched to the Wallaw where it was seen by 7,800 people. This has been the only time the society has produced two major musicals in the same year.

Blyth Operatic Society rehearsed for many years at the Blyth and District Social Club before moving to their present home in the Spartan Hotel. Each show programme carried a picture of the entire cast, dancers and production team. This was of the cast rehearsing Calamity Jane performed at the Wallaw Theatre in March 1971.

solution which certainly would not be condoned by the local authority or police nowadays.

Eddie Ferguson, a patron of the Society and head of the Ferguson's Transport firm, eventually bought the Wallaw when it was threatened with closure. He leased out the cinema side, with a certain written proviso to the effect the cinema had to be made available to the Blyth Operatic Society for performances at least twice a year. Eddie also improved the dressing room situation by having two changing rooms built easily accessible from the stage. Following his tragic death in a helicopter crash his wife, Laura, and elder son, Alan, have continued the family support of the amateur theatre. While no objection was raised to the rear stalls being converted into two mini cinemas in the 1980s, reducing the capacity of the Wallaw from 1,450 to 825, an attempt by Bob Milner, the lessee, to have the circle converted to two more cinemas was quickly quashed after an approach from the two societies to the Ferguson family. Bob, a real cinema buff was responsible, along with his chief projectionist Peter Douglas, for maintaining and adding to the art decor style of the building which even now attracts groups of cinema enthusiasts from all over the country.

In the early days of his tenancy Bob, a skilled musician, had an organ installed which he played to the patrons before the start of the films. Throughout his time in Blyth, before moving to Blackpool, Bob was the organist at St Mary's Church. In the meantime the Society extended the depth of the Wallaw stage twice until it is now twenty-two feet from the footlights to the back wall. The Proscenium arch, however, could not be moved which means the main curtains are now some ten feet from the footlights.

In the mid-1990s the problem of dismantling the screen was solved when a giant screen, which rolled up into the ceiling, was installed at a cost of £10,000. While it is still a difficult stage to work it is proving the lifeblood of the two major societies in the town as far as musicals are concerned. Both are prepared to invest in the building and in 1998 shared the cost, along with the owners, of re-carpeting the stalls. Members of both groups tackled the onerous job of lifting the old carpet which had been in since the cinema opened in 1937.

The members of Blyth Operatic Society once came to the aid of me and Radio Newcastle at the Tyneside Summer Exhibition. I was called in at an hour's notice to produce our programme from a large marquee

Ken Dodd was the star guest at the Blyth Operatic Society celebrity concert in September 1981, at the Wallaw. With the theatre packed the star had not appeared with fifteen minutes to go. The producer (the author) started to make emergency arrangements for stand-in turns and compere Bill Steel from Tyne Tees Television began to think of an apologetic speech. The operatic society chorus and soloists were already on stage when the comedian arrived from Blackpool where he was appearing in a summer show. As can be seen from the photograph the evening was undoubtedly a tremendous success.

January was the month members of Blyth Operatic Society charged their batteries in Spain prior to their major production in March. Favourite drinking haunt in Benidorm during the week long stay was Eduardos Music Bar where the tourists could be seen every lunchtime having an aperitif. The Society would give several concerts during their stay and had great difficulty on some occasions getting seats because word of mouth brought other holidaymakers out in force to listen to the music!

situated next to the Leazes Park lake after our star presenter, Frank Wappat, took ill. I arranged for guests to appear at very short notice on the afternoon show and also got together a cast from the Blyth Society for the concert in the evening. It was twenty minutes before the off at the concert with a packed marquee that we realised the organist had not turned up. I quickly rang him at home to discover the producer I had taken over from had not booked him for the concert and he was already engaged at a social club. I remembered a Newcastle organ firm was staging an exhibition further up the site and raced up there to chat to the musician demonstrating the organs. 'Do you read the dots,' I asked.

'Yes,' he replied.

An offer of £20 persuaded him to return with me to the marquee where it was five minutes to the off. Our first turn was Maurice Dobson, who apart from being a leading man with the Blyth Society had also been runner up in an *Opportunity Knocks* television programme. He was to open with the up-tempo number *Sweet Caroline*. He was duly introduced and walked on to an introduction to the song, which can only be described as 'multi-slow'. Maurice started beating out the time with his foot. I crept behind the organ and started beating out the time on the back of the instrument but the song progressed at the same pace. Eventually it finished. 'I thought you said you could read the dots,' I hissed to the player.

'I can,' he whispered back, 'but slowly.'

Fortunately for Maurice his other numbers went without a hitch and he was one of the successes of the evening.

A Blyth Operatic Society member whose ears should have been burning after the Radio Newcastle Tenth Anniversary concert one Saturday night in the City Hall was the secretary and tenor, Jimmy Bell. I produced the show, which drew capacity attendances at the two performances, and one of the featured acts was the chorus of the Blyth Society. We had already advertised that there would be a one hour programme broadcast of the show the following weekend.

It was when I got the master tape of the show to edit the programme the following Monday I realised I was in big trouble. The Operatic Society numbers were to be an integral part of the programme as a buffer between other turns but unfortunately the engineers had placed a microphone directly over Jimmy Bell, who was the strongest tenor in that section. As a result Jim's voice boomed out throughout all the numbers and that section of the tape was unusable. Fortunately, or unfortunately for the listeners, I was able to pad out the programme with a steel band which had been one of the acts.

The cast of Brigadoon performed by the Blyth Society at the Wallaw Cinema in 1968. The genuine piper at the back left is Bill Finlayson of Blyth and the men from left to right are: Bill Parker, Frank Scott, Brian Cook, Eddie Spark, Bill Thompson, Doug Matthews, the author, Colin Brown, Herbie Johnston and John Browell. The ladies of the chorus are (in alphabetical order): Anne Allen, Nell Archbold, Connie Brown, Christine Cook, Joyce Copping, Susan Dixon, Doreen Douglas, Kathleen Duffell, Irene Hannett, Rosemary Harland, Betty Hawkes, Emmie Johnston, Joy Jones, Marian Lambert, Rosalie Marsden, Nancy Martin, Mary Mason, Ruth Middleton, Ethel Parker, Ann Rix and Joan Waddle.

John Havis and John Bradley admire the vocal skills of the author during a performance of On the Twentieth Century *at the New Tyne Theatre, Newcastle, in 1981.*

Enid Bilton has played the leads in countless shows throughout the North East but does not seem particularly enamoured as the author croons to her in On the Twentieth Century *at the New Tyne Theatre, Newcastle, in 1981.*

The Merry Widow was the 1980 production of the Blyth Operatic Society at the Wallaw Cinema. Seen here, from left to right, are: Maurice Dobson, Phil Bainbridge, Geoff Marshall, Michael Goonan, Alf Douglas and Frank Scott.

The Phoenix Theatre Group

The birth of the Phoenix Theatre Group actually took place during the Second World War when the Phoenix Musical and Dramatic Society was formed in 1943. It made its home in the Miners' Welfare Hall in Renwick Road, now the Civic Centre. In keeping with those days and the high standing of aldermen and councillors the Society had the current mayor as president, the mayoress as vice-president and a councillor as chairman. The first play was *Burning Gold* quickly followed by *French Without Tears*. There is ample evidence the drama side flourished with as many as five plays in a season performed on the stage in what is now the Blyth Valley Council Chamber.

On one occasion two productions were staged on successive weeks. In the programme for George Bernard Shaw's *Arms and the Man*, producer Bobby Spark wrote:

'This is our 21st production. For a Society, which was only formed during the dark days of 1943, this is surely a proud record. May I look back a little? Do you remember our blackout curtains transformed into scenery? Our home-made lights? Shall I ever forget them? We owe a debt of gratitude to our stage managers of those days. Happy memories – Doreen Boyd winning a silver cup for her performance in Lottie Dundass, Nell Archbold as Madam Arcadi in Blithe Spirit and Eliza in Pygmalion and surely the funniest of all farces Women Aren't Angels, a world premiere of Alas Poor Yorick, and Kathleen MacReady, another cup winner, in Grief Goes Over, Jimmy Russell, a founder member, good in all parts, and a real trouper, Charlie Mills, Mary Dawson, Jimmy Tate, Winnie Durrant and Nora Kewen. So many memories crowding in but I must call a halt.'

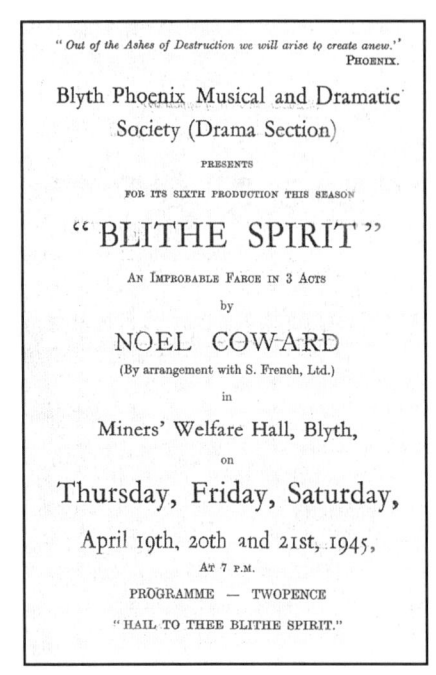

Blithe Spirit at the Miners' Welfare Hall, now the Civic Centre, was a triumph for Nell Archbold at Madam Arcadi who had already scored a tremendous success as Eliza in Shaw's Pygmalion.

While the drama side flourished the musical side did not. A concert version of *Merrie England* was staged in the Welfare Hall for two nights in 1945 on 29th March and 31st March conducted by John R. Johnson, who later helped revive Beaconsfield Operatic Society. Soloists were Edna Walker, Margaret Topping, John Searle and Harry Shuttleworth with Belle Haldane and 'Madam' Lizzie Long, as described in the programme, at the two pianos. Two of the Four Men of Windsor were Eddie

Spark and Jack Wilkinson who became founder members of the Blyth Society when it reformed in 1959.

By the time the twenty-first production was staged, *Arms and the Man* – the musical section was no longer and it was now the Blyth Phoenix Dramatic Society. Ambitious plans were being made by members to build their own theatre with a building fund already standing at £403 – a considerable amount in those days. It was this money which helped to build the Blyth Phoenix Theatre in Beaconsfield Street.

Productions fluctuated between the Welfare Hall and St Mary's Church Hall the leading lights at the time being Bill Elliott, John Stone, Charlie Russell, Jimmy Russell, Winnie Durrant, Alan Laws and Margaret Stitson. The Society eventually folded in the 1950s, shortly after I made my adult stage debut with them as a butler in *Dr Morelle*. I don't think I was responsible for the closure but there had been problems getting enough men to take part.

There was no trouble, however, getting men to turn out for the Phoenix cricket team which continued long after the Dramatic Society was abandoned. The team continued into the late 1960s playing

The cast of the Blyth Phoenix Dramatic Society production of Dr Morelle at the Welfare Hall (now the Civic Centre) in 1953. Back row, left to right: The author, Jimmy Woollen, Bill Elliott, Jimmy Russell. Front row: Peter Vlieland (a South African reporter working for the Blyth News), Irene Robinson, Margaret Stitson and Charles Russell.

friendly matches every weekend up and down Northumberland and Durham. Several of the now redundant actors took part but in the main the standard of play was not of the highest and it was love of the game which kept them at it.

For some reason the team's fixture list included games at a number of mental hospitals where you had to be escorted through locked doors to the changing rooms. One memorable match was at Northgate Hospital just outside Morpeth where we had an escort back to the pitch through crowds of patients after changing into our whites. On one occasion the Northgate team, unknown to us, included a patient who seemed completely normal. We only realised he was an inmate when he took a rather violent turn after being given out and had to be escorted by two male nurses back to his locked quarters. Later he joined us for tea where he was perfectly normal and lucid thanks to having received his medication. We also had matches at two other mental institutions – St George's Hospital at Stannington and St Nicholas' Hospital in Gosforth – beautiful grounds but one could not help feel sorry for the unfortunates who were patients.

The highlight of our trips, though, was not the cricket but the after-match entertainment. We travelled by coach and were able to pick and choose the hostelries for the nights drinking. Once our batsman-cum-pianist, Benny Cobb, was persuaded to tinkle the ivories there was no lack of singing. Indeed there was so much talent in the side we were able to form the Phoenix Concert Party, which did several engagements for charity.

The Phoenix Building Fund was still in existence but had to lay in the bank gathering interest as it could only be touched if used for the original purpose. Enter Councillor Mrs Renee Gallon who was the driving force behind the formation of Blyth Arts and Community Association. It used the former Methodist Church in Beaconsfield Street as its headquarters and also as a venue for money-raising shows on its limited stage. She was able to gain access to the building fund, which now stood at £600, by entering into an agreement to name the building the Phoenix Theatre. There was a desperate need to raise funds to develop the church as a fully blown theatre and to this end I decided to stage a special production of the musical *The Sound of Music* at the Wallaw in October 1973.

The Blyth Valley Operatics came into being for the one show only and got the fullest support from Beaconsfield Operatic Society which was, at that time, using the Phoenix as its rehearsal base. Trevor Harder was appointed chairman, Bill Parker, treasurer, Howard Davison musical director, Alan Smith, accompanist and I became production director and secretary. Choreographer was Barbara Lawton, singing coach was Kathleen Parker, later to join the Royal Opera House, and board members included Norman Counden, Howard Davison, Tom Easton, David Ferrow, David Garrett and Alan Smith. Wives were also roped in with Doreen Smith and Rosemary Harland acting as booking secretaries – a job which turned out to be one of the busiest. Jennie

McManners, formerly with Doyle Carte was 'borrowed' from Gateshead Operatic Society to play Maria and Sheila Stewart from Tynemouth Operatic Society took the part of Elsa Schraeder.

Because of the limited depth of the stage, it was still twelve feet at the time, David Garrett and I designed a convenient set, which worked on the principal of independent tabs (curtains). When the rope was pulled half the tabs opened while the other half closed. In this way the interior of the abbey and Von Trapp's home could be accessed in double quick time. George Colpitts, a former town councillor and president of the Blyth Operatic Society, built, free of charge, a moveable staircase in steel and wood which was wheeled in from the wings while an eight-feet high set of windows, complete with drapes, was carried in to be positioned in front of the half tab covering the abbey altar.

Blyth Co-operative Society, thanks to the generosity of general manager Harold Whitehead, provided a new three-piece suite while Father Thomas Power made sure an incense burner was rushed to the theatre after the Sunday morning service at St Wilfrid's Church for use in the show. The show, unfortunately, got off to a bad start – not on stage but in the circle where an elderly lady collapsed and died on the opening night just as the overture started up. Others during the week could also have suffered heart attacks when the Nazi guards hunting for the Von Trapp family in the auditorium got a bit too enthusiastic and started manhandling patrons. Fortunately it was all taken 'in the best possible taste'.

The Sound of Music was an outstanding success and set an attendance record for the Wallaw by pulling in 8,141 patrons who paid only 40 pence and 30 pence a ticket. Even so, a cheque for £500 was presented to Mrs Gallon for the Phoenix Building fund by Trevor Harder after the final performance. It was still many years before a new £1 million theatre was to rise on the site, thanks to a £750,000 grant from the National Lottery, but unfortunately Mrs Gallon was not able to see her dream realised as she had passed on.

Jenny McManners, who starred in the 1973 special production of The Sound of Music in aid of the Blyth Arts Council is seen here (top left) with her husband, Dr Joseph McManners, and the author and his wife, Rosemary. Jenny unfortunately passed away in 2001 after a long illness.

Putting on a full scale musical like The Sound of Music on a twelve foot deep stage at the Wallaw in 1973 was fraught with problems but the author (left), assisted by David Garrett came up with a solution which worked perfectly and was seen by a record attendance for the week.

Seven of the nuns who sang in the Blyth Valley Operatic's production of The Sound of Music in 1973 in aid of the Blyth Arts and Community Association Phoenix Theatre Building Fund. From left to right: Rosalie Marsden, Sheila Black, Jaqueline Hoult, Angela Pearcey, Freida Reid, Gloria Carroll and Vivienne Jackson.

Jennie McManners (Maria) with the children on stage during a performance of The Sound of Music in 1973. The children, from left to right, are: Carol Parker (Gretl), Christine Ferrow (Marta), Janet Harland (Brigitta), Aubrey Smith (Kurt), June Tosney (Louisa), Brian Cook (Friedrich) and Jaqueline Lambert (Liesl).

Ridley Park, Blyth, was the setting for this photograph of Maria and the Von Trapp children in the 1973 production of The Sound of Music at the Wallaw Cinema. Back row, from left to right, are: Jacqueline Lambert, Brian Cook, Aubrey Smith, Janet Harland and June Tosney. Front row: Carol Parker, Jennie McManners and Christine Ferrow.

Several operatic societies provided the cast and backstage crew, under the title of Blyth Valley Operatics, for the special production of The Sound of Music at the Wallaw in 1973. The photo for the programme was taken at the rear of Delaval Hall.

SECTION FIVE

THE ENTERTAINERS

One of the most popular events before the Second World War was the Blyth Carnival. It was held during the summer and boasted a King and Queen (always played by a man) and Jester. Jimmy Luke (centre) was the permanent Jester. Unfortunately there is no record of the names of his two Royal colleagues in this picture believed to have been taken in the early 1930s.

Jimmy Russell was a person who featured regularly in the life of Blyth for almost forty years from the Second World War. Not only was he a splendid actor, who once trod the boards professionally for a short period, but he was also the finest comedian, or shall we say comic raconteur, in the area. Until the advent of television nearly every pit village or town boasted a comic entertainer who had his own style and fund of personal jokes. There was Fred Bailey from Backworth, who also had a fine tenor voice, and Jimmy Munro of Stakeford whose trademark was a false black moustache and a flat cap and who opened his act by saying, 'I was lying in bed the other day chopping sticks.' Blyth boasted Jimmy Luke, who was a visual comic and the Town Jester for many years at the now sadly defunct Blyth Carnival, and Jimmy Russell.

Jimmy, although a Geordie, spoke 'proper' but was brilliantly able to convey any type of accent with which he littered his stories. One of my favourites concerned the naval revue off Spithead attended by the British, American and Russian navies. The respective admirals got together on board the British flagship and after an inspection of assembled crews started a discussion on courage. The Russian admiral claimed his men were the bravest and called forward Ivan Ivanovic

The principal cast of The New Moon – Blyth Operatic Society's 1962 production at the Theatre Royal – took themselves off to the South Harbour at Blyth for publicity pictures. From left to right: Walter McEvoy, Jimmy Bell, the author and Jimmy Russell.

from his men assembled on deck. 'Climb eighty feet into the rigging and dive,' he ordered. Ivan snapped off a salute, climbed the rigging and dived.

'There,' said the Russian admiral, 'that's Russian courage.'

'You ain't seen nothing,' said the American admiral. 'Hey Spike, come here.'

Spike ambled forward. 'Yeah, what do you want Joe?'

'Climb ninety feet into the rigging and dive.'

'Sure thing,' said Spike who climbed the rigging and dove.

'There,' said the admiral, 'that's American courage.'

'Very good show, very good show,' said the British admiral. 'Able Seaman Smith step forward.' Able Seaman Smith stepped forward.

'Climb 100 feet into the rigging and dive.'

Able Seaman Smith looked slowly up the mast. 'Dive your bloody self,' he said.

'Now that,' said the Admiral, 'is what I call courage."

An offshoot of the Blyth Phoenix Dramatic Society was the Phoenix Cricket club and an offshoot of the cricket club was the Phoenix Concert party which gave shows in aid of charity. Pictured here at the Wellesley Nautical School – a merchant navy training establishment in Blyth for rather wayward young gentlemen – are, back row: Jimmy Woollen, Eddie Legg, John Hickman, the author, Bill Elliott, Charlie Russell, Billy Cook, Bob Millican. Front row: Benny Cobb, Jack Anderson, Alf Douglas, Jimmy Young, Doreen Douglas and Jack Allen.

Jimmy was always in demand and appeared in a large number of concert parties, which toured the clubs in the post-war years. In a way the concert party scene reflected the professional variety circuit with a number of acts, one after the other, winding up with a finale featuring the entire cast. He regularly appeared with Four Kings and a Joker, which also featured Frankie Riley, Blyth's outstanding silken voiced crooner. The party travelled the clubs in Northumberland and Durham for many years. Another party was the Gimmecracks composed of Alan Hetherington, who was also a well known local soccer referee, Jack Allen, who was leader of Blyth Town Boys' Clubs and who deservedly was awarded the BEM for his services on his retirement, and Alan Millican. Alan was later to become part of the Millican and Nesbit duo which consistently won Hughie Green's *Opportunity Knocks* on television, success which took them to the London Palladium and into the Top Twenty hit records.

Alan was a most modest man. I can recall bumping into him in Newcastle when he was at the height of his fame and he introduced me to his wife as, 'Jim Harland. You know. The singer.' This was in reference to my efforts on the amateur operatic stage.

Flower and vegetable shows were a feature in the life of members of the Waterloo Social Club. Seen here about to present the cup to one of the winners at a show in the 1930s is Mrs Mary McSherry, whose husband Ted – or Pop as he was occasionally known – is the gentleman standing second left.

Mrs Mary McSherry, wife of the first steward of the Waterloo Social Club pictured in the 1930s with Mr Wilkinson, one of the judges at the club's annual flower show. Note the pencil behind his ear and the blooms all placed in beer bottles.

Unfortunately Alan and his partner, Tommy, were not able to benefit financially long term from their national success. Everyone seemed to be getting a cut of the money pouring in other than the singers themselves.

When fame subsided Tommy took himself off to Australia while Alan got a job at an ironworks at Seaton Delaval and sang occasionally in the clubs. On his early death there was a tremendous turn out at his funeral.

Jimmy Russell was also secretary of the Waterloo Social Club. The club, when I initially joined it in 1959, was situated in Meldrum House, a Victorian three-storied building. The 'lounge' was the small kitchen with a large fireplace on which, no doubt, the meals had been cooked. Every Sunday lunchtime several of us, all members of the Blyth Operatic Society, would meet for drinks. The party consisted of musicians Brian Lambert, Norman Waddle and Gerald O'Connell, headmaster and JP, Gerald Kelly and myself. While the Sunday lunchtime gathering still takes place, I am the last surviving member of the original gang.

In those days you could go out with ten bob – that's 50 pence nowadays – buy a round of drinks and still have change, which is indicative of the cost of living then. 'Mine Host' was Ted McSherry Jnr, one of the great characters of the town who followed his father, Ted Snr, who served twenty-seven years as the first steward of the club. Ted Jnr had converted the large garden at the front of the club into two big chicken runs with wire mesh fencing on either side of the path leading to the main entrance. He kept a large number of hens which provided not only him and his family but also many club members with free range treats. The hens were also a source of amusement to members. On one occasion a member strode into the bar with birds under each arm, put them on the counter, and told Ted, 'Your sign's fallen down.'

I am afraid I am the one who led to Ted losing all his hens - and to the demolition of Meldrum House and the building of the existing Waterloo Social Club. It came about when I was working in Newcastle for the *Evening Chronicle*. Twice a week teams consisting of a reporter, photographer and a driver were sent out on what we called the 'overnight runs'. The purpose was for the team to collect three or four stories which could be kept overnight for use when there was a shortage of copy or to fill pages set a day in advance. On this occasion I brought my team to Blyth and to the club. There we took photographs of drinkers standing at the entrance looking at the hens, which were perched very nicely on the mesh wire fences. Ted and his hens provided a nice little human interest story which duly appeared two days later. Within twenty-four hours of publication, Ted was visited by the Blyth Borough Council health inspector who told him in no uncertain terms the hens had to go. This was followed by a comprehensive examination of the premises which led to the committee deciding to invest in a new club rather than spend the thousands needed to bring the existing one up to scratch. When Ted died after twenty-three years service his wife, Madge, carried on for two years as stewardess and the family connection has been continued by his daughter, Christine, who is relief stewardess there.

A mention of Jackie Allen earlier brought back memories of my time as a member of the Blyth Town Boys' Club which was based in Wright Street. Jack, who was club leader, was possibly responsible for me getting the nickname of 'Hank'.

I was working as a junior reporter on the *Morpeth Herald* at the time but in my evenings off I was a regular at the club. Jack suggested I might like to launch a news sheet as he had a battered old typewriter, a ink duplicator and a spare cupboard under the stairs leading to the hall above. Shortly after the first edition came out the nickname started to be used. Why, I asked Jack, had I suddenly acquired it. His reply was, 'After Hank Jansen.'

Hank Jansen, at that time, was the favourite author of the older boys. His paperbacks in the early 1950s were regarded as pornography in those days, although they would be regarded as extremely tame now. I am pleased to say the nickname did not last too long.

Another member, Alan Murray, and I brought out regular issues of the newsheet which occasionally included attacks on a group of older

Ted McSherry, steward of the Waterloo Social Club, feeds his hens watched by members of the club. Three days later he was told by Blyth Council to get rid of the birds as they were a health hazard. The man responsible was the author (second left) who published a light-hearted story in the Evening Chronicle in 1962.

boys in the club – one in particular who gave younger members a hard time riding roughshod over their rights. Our paths have crossed a number of times in adulthood as we both live in Blyth and I still can't stand him. Mind you the feeling is reciprocated.

It was through the Boys' Club I made my first trip and fell in love with Ford Castle, that beautiful and peaceful estate in North Northumberland close to Flodden Field, the scene of the great battle between the Scots and the English. I attended a National Association of Boys' Club training week during which we were visited by the then president of the association, the Duke of Gloucester, who was amazed when I presented him at the end of his short visit with a newsheet reporting full details of his tour. Little did he realise the whole report had been typed up in advance and could have been given to him as he arrived. Royal visits stick rigidly to the written schedule! Later in my career I would write and commentate on visits to Northumberland and Newcastle by Princess Alexandra, Princess Margaret and the Queen and Prince Phillip.

The author, aged sixteen, (front row right) on the steps leading to the main entrance of Ford Castle where he spent happy times on National Association of Boys Club courses. It was there he was introduced to the then Duke of Gloucester and presented the astonished Royal with the course newspaper he had edited detailing his visit to the castle.

SECTION SIX

THE RED SHADOW

The first picture of the author in the Red Shadow costume for the 1963 Blyth production of The Desert Song. It was to be worn by him at four more venues – The Forum, Hexham; The Theatre Royal, Newcastle; Silksworth Community Centre, Sunderland and the Solingen Town Theatre in Germany before it was laid to rest.

The year 1952 saw one of the first party of young people from Blyth travelling to the new twin town of Solingen in Germany. It was led by Miss Valerie Tully (in the shiny coat) who was the Northumberland County Council youth service co-ordinator. The author, who was chairman of Blyth Youth Council at the time, is the one immediately behind Miss Tully's head. He was to return 13 years later to sing the lead in The Desert Song at the Solingen theatre.

Ned Breadin, a long-serving Blyth councillor, was lying in a bed in a side ward of Wansbeck Hospital in Ashington when I spotted him. I was on my way to visit a relative but popped in to see how he was. Sitting in the ward was his daughter and he introduced us saying, 'This is the Red Shadow.' The year was 2000 and Ned, who is now in the great council chamber in the sky, was referring to a part I played in *The Desert Song* at the old Theatre Royal in Blyth in 1963.

Some years earlier I knocked on the door of a house my wife and I were hoping to buy in Blyth to be welcomed by a lady with the words, 'Oh, the Red Shadow.' She eventually sold us the house where we still reside.

No matter how many leads in shows I have since played, some twenty-five or so including the romantic Emile de Becque in *South Pacific*, the older generation of the town seems only to remember that Sigmund Romberg musical.

Why *The Desert Song* holds such memories is a mystery. It is the story of a Frenchman, the son of a colonial governor, who becomes the disguised leader of a band of Riffs, the Robin Hoods of their day, seeking to rid the country of the French. What is certain is that the public wallowed in the escapism of the Shadow kidnapping a beautiful girl and carrying her off into the desert. And in the beautiful and memorable score and action involving marching soldiers, harem girls and a band of singing bandits.

The show was written in the 1920s by Sigmund Romberg after a best selling book was turned into the Rudolf Valentino's silent film *The Sheik*. Since then it has been performed thousands of times throughout the world. The English tenor John Hanson made a very good living out of it touring Britain every two years or so. Now Hanson was not the greatest actor in the world by a long chalk, in fact he was quite poor, but he was Olivier compared to the performance of a singer called David Whitfield. David was a very handsome, blond, popular English tenor who had a number of Top Twenty hits to his credit, the most famous being *Cara Mia* and *Everywhere*. But he should have left acting well alone if his Red Shadow at the Empire Theatre in Newcastle was anything to go by.

Blyth Operatic Society last performed *The Desert Song* in 1934 with the lead being played by Bill Robinson. As that was before I was born I naturally did not have a chance to see it but by all accounts he did an excellent job. As soon as I landed the role comparisons with Bill were being made as a few of the chorus members had appeared in the pre-war production. The 1963 show had Pearl Powell as Margot, Gerald Kelly as General Birabeau, Jimmy Russell as the comedian, Benny, with Nancy Haxon as his sidekick, Susan, Bob Young, a fine tenor, as Sid El Kar and Jack Wilkinson, a tremendous bass, as Ali Ben Ali.

There were not too many problems although the donkey, which was needed to bring Benny in on his entrance, steadfastly refused to enter the stage door of the theatre. At least it saved us the embarrassment suffered during a romantic scene in *White Horse Inn* when a goat did its business on the stage. For some reason the stage manager wanted the mess cleaned up and he sent on the diminutive Fred Turnbull, then 14, and later to become a six foot centre half with Aston Villa, with a broom and shovel. Unfortunately he did the job as Mildred Eadington,

'As stubborn as a mule' goes the saying but it also applied to a certain donkey to be used in one scene in The Desert Song at the Theatre Royal in 1963. The animal did not fancy using the narrow stage door and nothing would coax it through. It spent the week chewing grass in a field along the Blyth Links!

playing Josepha, and I were singing a romantic duet and the audience saw the funny side of it.

White Horse Inn had been a sell-out and so indeed was the week long run of *The Desert Song*.

Two years later it was decided to take a show to Blyth's twin town of Solingen. Our current production of *The Vagabond King* was not deemed suitable so *The Desert Song* was revived, In retrospect it was a tremendous undertaking with a cast of over 60 having to be transported by coach to Newcastle, train to London, coach to Dover, boat to Ostend, train to Cologne then coach to Solingen. In addition all cast members had to carry their own costumes. Howard Davison was to play Ali Ben Ali and had been sent a magnificent, newly made, outfit by Mutries of Edinburgh, one of the top stage costumiers. It was while we were unpacking the coaches in Solingen that Howard realised he had left his costume on the train, which was now deep in East Germany. The costume was never seen again and Howard had to wear a make-do-and-mend effort from the wardrobe mistress for the two performances of the show.

It was during our train trip from Ostend to Cologne that Gerald Kelly, who was to reprise the role of General Birabeau, showed a side of his nature we never knew existed. Gerald had been an officer in the army of occupation in Germany after the war and had been instrumental in helping with the twinning of Blyth with Solingen. It was during the train trip that two drunken Americans came into the section of the

Rallying the Riffs. The Red Shadow (the author) and Sid el Kar (Bob Young) singing the famous Riff Song on the Theatre Royal stage in March, 1963.

And taking their bow at the end of what proved to be a highly successful performance are the Red Shadow and Margot (Pearl Powell).

train, which was the old fashioned type with a corridor, occupied by the cast. They began behaving in a belligerent way and started to frighten the women in the party. Gerald sat quietly in the corner seat for a while then suddenly jumped up, ran out of the carriage, grabbed one of the Yanks bodily by the collar and seat of his pants, raced him twenty yards down the corridor and threw him against the panelling. He then opened the door and pushed the Americans into the next carriage and locked the door. Gerald then quietly turned and resumed his seat. The two Americans were thrown off the train at the next stop without their belongings.

The arrival in Solingen, where we were to stay with German families, proved somewhat of a cultural shock. There were still signs of the bombing the steel town had taken but it was the theatre, which took our breath away. It was huge with a concert hall attached. The dressing rooms had wall to wall mirrors and showers and an ultra modern tannoy system. Thinking of our Theatre Royal – cold water, flooded boiler room, leaky roof and closed gallery I just had to comment, 'And we won the war.'

Renee Gallon, the producer, almost had a fit when she found the huge stage was bare of scenery. Two stagehands then wheeled on a large paper-machete rock, the entrance to the Shadow's cave. 'Is that all,' she said.

'Wait,' replied the German stage manager. He walked over to a lighting board and with a flick of a few switches transformed the stage into a perfect setting for the first scene The two performances of the show, an afternoon one for schoolchildren and an evening one the following day for adults, were a tremendous success. We had doubts initially whether our English version would be understood. Jimmy Russell's first entrance as Benny would give us the answer. When gales of laughter came over the tannoy in the dressing room we knew we were on a winner.

The following day Jimmy popped into a shop in the town and was immediately recognised as Benny by the staff who refused to take any money for the cigarettes and gifts he bought. When I went out into town I could hear the murmur of 'Rote Schatten' from passers by – the Red Shadow in German. We understood later why we had made such an impression. Such a production was unique. There was no such thing as a German amateur operatic society or indeed any professional company touring musicals.

My wife, Rosemary, young daughter, Janet, and I along with Brian Lambert the musical director, his wife, Marion and daughter, Jacqueline, stayed with Charlie Weiden and his wife in a rather large house. Charlie, who was slightly disabled, had been in the Werhmacht during the war on guard duty at Cologne Railway Station. He was not prepared to talk of his experiences. He admitted being a supporter of Hitler who, he said, did a lot of good for Germany when he took over. He provided full employment, built the autobahns and the 'People's car'. Like most Germans at that time he denied any knowledge of the persecution of the Jews shrugging his shoulders when I suggested he must have known the cattle trucks which passed through the station carried human beings. But they were splendid hosts and there were tears when we had to leave.

The year 1965 marked a landmark in the history of Blyth Operatic Society when more than 60 members travelled to Solingen in Germany to give two performance of The Desert Song. Thanks to the extensive publicity by means of posters and radio adverts in the steel town both shows were sold out.

Städtefreundschaft Solingen - Blyth/England

Gastspiel der
Blyth Operatic Society

im Theater der Stadt Solingen
in Gemeinschaft mit der
Theatergesellschaft „Wohlgemuth", Solingen,

am DIENSTAG, dem 15. JUNI 1965, 20.00 Uhr:

The Desert Song
(Das Lied der Wüste)

Operette in englischer Sprache in zwei Akten von Otto Harbach, Oskar Hammerstein
und Frank Mandel   Musik von Sigmund Romberg
Regie: Mrs. Renee Gallon   Musikalische Leitung: Albert Lawton

Kartenvorverkauf: Eintrittspreise: 2,00 bis 4,00 DM
Zigarrenhaus Mühlensiepen, Hauptstraße, Ecke Linkgasse · Gaststätte Kropp, Potsdamer Straße · Theaterkasse ab 8. Juni 1965

Die Aufführung wird am Mittwochnachmittag, 16. Juni 1965, 16.00 Uhr, für die englischsprechenden Schüler der Solinger Schulen wiederholt.
Der Eintrittspreis für diese Vorstellung beträgt einheitlich 1,50 DM · Kartenvorverkauf durch die Theaterkasse ab 8. Juni 1965

The visit of Blyth Operatic Society to Solingen in Germany was a highlight of 1965. Unfortunately very few pictures exist of the actual performance of The Desert Song but this one shows the Red Shadow (the author), Ali Ben Ali (Howard Davison) and Sid el Kar (Bob Young) in the Eastern Western love trio.

My Red Shadow mask lay dormant for four years then I accepted an invitation to play the role for the Hexham Amateur Stage Society and it was there during one of the performances I took to the stage as Pierre looking like a Beatle. The show calls upon the Red Shadow to divest himself of his costume and re-appear as the general's son in twenty seconds. This means a split second costume change in the darkness of the wings. Everything went right the first two nights with the stage wig I was wearing as Pierre being the last thing to be put on. On this occasion I dashed back on the stage and as the scene progressed I could see great hilarity in the wings. Somehow I sensed I was the reason for it. Casually lifting my hand I felt the back of the wig and realised it had been put on back to front. Fortunately it was a short scene and I was able to back off at my exit finding it extremely hard not to break into a smile.

However, when the invitation came for me to guest for the Newcastle and District Operatic Society's production at the Theatre Royal in Newcastle I was determined such an occurrence would not happen again. There was a firm specialising in hairpieces in Eldon Square and I persuaded the owner to lend me a ready-made hairpiece for the duration of the show. This was kept in place by double-sided adhesive and meant the saving of precious seconds in the quick-change scene. Unfortunately, I succumbed to the flattery of some of the chorus girls who said I should wear it permanently as it suited me. Like a fool I did and so it stayed like a dead rat on my bald pate for thirty years – a terrible inconvenience when swimming, playing cricket and refereeing. It was discarded forever when I accepted the role of the completely bald Daddy Warbucks in *Annie* for the Blyth Society at the Wallaw in 1999.

My final appearance as the Red Shadow came in 1972 when I accepted another invitation this time to perform in Sunderland for a local society. At last, I thought, I would achieve an ambition to act on the stage of the Sunderland Empire. Alas it turned out to be in a Community Centre. It was when I looked out at the audience, during a singing of *One Alone* I realised this would be my farewell to the part. And so it has proved.

The author (Pierre) and Gerald Kelly (General Birabeau) in a scene from The Desert Song at the Theatre Royal in 1963. The two reprised the parts in Solingen, Germany, two years later.

SECTION SEVEN

A CAREER IN JOURNALISM AND BROADCASTING

The 1985 Milk Cup Final between Sunderland and Norwich City saw the author producing a live programme from Wembley Stadium. He carried out interviews on the pitch with leading personalities and then had to dash for the Press Box when the teams came out before kick-off as he was also commentating on the match. He found himself in the reception room of the Royal Box as he headed up the main stand. Fortunately it was empty at the time – the Royal personages having taken their seats – and he was able to find his way out!

The Blyth News

The *Blyth News and Ashington Post* was undoubtedy the most popular local paper in East Northumberland. It had to be – it was the only one apart from the *Ashington Advertiser* which circulated only in Ashington. When I joined the reporting staff from the *Morpeth Herald* in 1953 at the age of eighteen the editor was Bill Hogg who was in charge of several staff in Blyth and also controlled the office in Station Road, Ashington. The paper was editionised, that is the front page with a different mast-head carried news from Ashington and Newbiggin which could not be read in the Blyth edition and vice versa. It was early 1953 and the newspaper in those days was published twice a week, on Mondays and Thursdays. The fact that you had to pay for the paper meant editorial content held sway over the commercial side with no more than a third of the paper being turned over to advertising. Today, unfortunately, the opposite is the case although understandable as the successor to the *Blyth News*, the *News Post Leader*, is a free sheet and advertising has to pay all the costs.

The two-storied offices were in Waterloo Road, later taken over by the North Eastern Electricity Board, and now occupied by a charity shop. On the ground floor Ronnie Orr, the office manager, Ronnie George his deputy and a female assistant handled the advertising side. Upstairs was the reporters' room, the sub-editor's room, the editor's office and the photographic dark room – the sole province of staff photographer, Ray Dunn. The Ashington office in Station Road was manned by senior reporter Tom Chape and a manageress.

Blyth boasted a large reporting staff as the Monday edition meant staff having to work weekends – five and half-day weeks for the journalists. There were five reporters and a chief reporter while the subbing was done by John Hogg, brother of Bill, who also assisted with the subbing at pressure times and the sports content was in the hands of Bob Thompson, who wrote under 'Crofter' – adopted from his regular attendance at Croft Park, home of Blyth Spartans.

One of Bill's jobs was to write the editorial twice a week but despite my tender years I discovered he passed this job out to anyone who did not seem too busy. This meant the papers opinion was expressed on my typewriter on many occasions.

The arrival of John Kirk, a rather colourful character from Northampton, in the reporters' room led me to have my first active involvement with the free enterprise culture. One morning John and I were having coffee in Newman's, which was above Newman's bakers shop in Waterloo Road. It was a good source of news tip-offs being frequented most mornings by the numerous insurance men working in Blyth. The premises are now Pal Joey's ladies and gents clothing shop. I told him I had an idea to make money by opening a second hand motor cycle shop in the town. Having recently passed my motor cycle driving test and knowing the difficulty in obtaining a cheap bike I was interested in providing a service to others that found themselves in the same boat. The initial cash for the launch, I told him, would be the bugbear. Now John was one of the most untidy dressers I have ever come across with coat and pants pockets bulging. With what, I did not know until that morning. 'No problem,' he said, as he proceeded to unload scores and scores of National Savings certificates from his pockets.

'How much have you got there?' I asked.

He had no idea and we proceeded to count them. Now bear in mind we were only on about four pounds a week. John, I discovered, had £700 worth of certificates. My query about where the money had come from fell on deaf ears, Anyhow that was how John and I went into partnership and rented a one-roomed shop in Regent Street near to the now demolished Traveller's Rest pub. I have a fancy it is what is now John's Chinese Takeaway but so much demolition has taken place in that area I cannot be certain. We advertised in our own paper for second hand bikes and bought half a dozen from the replies. These were taken to a mechanic who put them in a road-worthy condition and the business was launched. Four of them went in two days during the evening hours we were open. One pound down and 14 weekly payments of the same amount was the deal. On each bike we were making a profit of £5.

Again we advertised for more stock and on this occasion we got a call from an elderly gentleman in Newsham. He had a motorcycle and sidecar for sale but was unable to drive it to us as he felt he was too old to go back on the roads. John and I visited the old chap and he took us to a shed in his back garden and there, under a tarpaulin cover, was a magnificent machine complete with sidecar, gear change on the petrol tank and carbide gas lamps! It was a 1922 model in full working order which he had maintained with love and affection over the years. We paid him £15 for it and I drove it to the shop.

The following day John and I were due to attend our weekly shorthand and journalists training course at the South Shields Marine and Technical College and I hit on the idea of forsaking the bus and travelling in our new acquisition. John was all for the idea and so it was he sat proudly in the open green sidecar while I steered the vehicle

---

'Phone Blyth 35.

For Value and Variety

Shop at

J. Newman's

BAKER AND PASTRY COOK

3, WATERLOO ROAD, BLYTH,

& STATION RD., ASHINGTON.

Fresh Cream Cakes
a Speciality.

An advert for Newman's.

along the coast road, through Whitley Bay and Tynemouth and down to the North Shields ferry. We drove up to the college, congratulated ourselves on getting there in less than half the normal time and went in for our lessons. What we had forgotten was that it would be dark when our classes were over. And it was also pouring with rain. No lights – no journey home.

We then began a hunt for carbide pellets which would provide the gas to allow us to use the lighting system on the bike. Now in those days carbide was in regular use rather like the small camping gas cylinders nowadays. It was not difficult to buy a tin in a local shop for a few pence. We also obtained a bottle, which we filled with the water needed to start the gas emitting from the pellets. The system worked on the principle of water slowly dripping from the upper level of a two-compartment metal container on to the carbide and the gas flowing along rubber tubing to lamps on the front and rear and sidecar.

We duly followed the instructions and wasted half a box of matches and half an hour trying to get the lamps ignited. We tried again, increasing the amount of carbide and getting thoroughly frustrated as the rain soaked even further into our clothes. The rest of the matches were spent. John bought another box. By now we had been trying for an hour to get out of the middle of South Shields, I was due to cover Seaton Valley Urban Council in two hours time and was getting a little perturbed.

'Look,' I said to John. 'Let's pour the rest of the carbide in the bottom section and instead of allowing the water to drip pour all the water directly on to it.'

John agreed. And so it was when we lit the match a gigantic flame leapt from the metal mixing container between the bike and sidecar. Fortunately for us the rain did a fireman's job before it could do any serious damage.

How did we get home? We bought a hand torch and John, sitting in the sidecar, pointed it to the front or the rear according to my instructions! For the life of me I cannot remember what happened to the machine but I only wish we had mothballed it, as it would be worth a fortune nowadays.

Our business was brought to an end after our employers informed us they thought it was not in their interests for us to have two occupations.

My second spell on the *Blyth News* came in 1958 when Ronnie Cross was the editor. The paper now came out weekly on a Thursday and had moved from Waterloo Road to Regent Street. The reporters' room, on the first floor, overlooked the Police Box in the Market Place, long since disappeared along with the numerous policemen who were around in those days. One of my colleagues was Allan Powell, later to be news editor of Tyne Tees Television and currently Teesside reporter for BBC *Look North*. Chief reporter was the large, towering Andy Easton who had moved to Blyth from the *Alnwick Gazette*.

My outstanding memory of Allan Powell was when he was entrusted with the brand new *Blyth News* van in which to do his Bedlington calls. He parked in the Front Street and returned to find it had run down the hill and crashed into the Market Cross. It was out of action for a couple of weeks and Allan had to face the wrath of both Ronnie and Andy.

One of the more unusual stories I was involved in was when I investigated an alleged poltergeist at a terraced house in Hastings Terrace, New Hartley. It was occupied by a retired miner and his wife along with his daughter, son-in-law and small granddaughter. I had stumbled on the story accidentally when I heard there was a house in the village where a mysterious pounding noise on a partitioning wall could be heard but not felt. The family was not keen on any publicity but eventually I persuaded them to tell of the strange goings-on in their home. Boiling eggs were apparently being lifted out of the bubbling pan and placed on the draining board and glass marbles were being propelled out of a vase across the room. In addition there was the pounding sound on the internal wall which the whole family had heard. I carried out the interviews during the day and as the strange happenings took place mainly at night I decided to return to the house bringing with me my fellow reporter John Ritson. I may say that as soon as we entered we both had a feeling that something strange was there. It was cold, although the coal fire was on, and the hairs were standing on the back of my neck. It was while we were talking to the old miner I caught a glimpse of something silvery moving swiftly at a low height towards me from the direction of the kitchen door. I was struck just above the knee and on looking down saw a spoon lying on the floor. There was no logical explanation as to how it happened and the following Thursday we carried the story with both our names on the by-line. When the young couple and child moved to another house the troubles stopped.

Marriage and a much larger pay packet led to me leaving the *Blyth News* and joining the *Evening Chronicle* in Newcastle.

Seen here at his desk in Thomson House, Newcastle, while working with the Journal is the author.

The Eddie Milne Era

The adoption meeting of a certain Edward Milne at the Bedlington Market Place Club heralded the beginning of a stormy period for the Blyth Constituency Labour Party. I was one of several journalists who took part in his first press conference after he had been chosen and I must say he gave the impression of being an affable Scot who was seeking to establish good relations with the media.

Wilf Holliday was the full time agent based at the constituency party offices and Labour Rooms in Seaforth Street, Blyth, above the Blyth and Tyne pub. He was the right hand man as far as sitting MP Alf Robens was concerned and with him being in the Cabinet all local affairs and appointments were left to Wilf. Alf's resignation to become head of the National Coal Board came as a shock but was then warmly welcomed by the local NUM. The union believed he would look after their interests. As it happened they were to be disappointed. Favours were granted to nobody as he tackled the increasing problems of an industry way behind the times. Some years earlier Alf had confided to Bob Gordon, a journalist colleague of mine, in the Guide Post Workingmen's Club he was a professional politician and could easily have served the 'other side'.

Immediately opposite the Labour Rooms were the district premises of the Newcastle *Evening Chronicle*, *Journal* and *Sunday Sun* where I worked. My first floor office was opposite that belonging to Wilf and indeed I regularly popped across for a coffee with him. We discussed everything – other than Labour Party affairs. It soon became noticeable to me that Wilf felt he was being under used by the new MP and less than a year after his election Wilf told me his was more a part-time job now. Eddie Milne's fault was he could not delegate. He was a hands on person and also one who could not take criticism as I found on the two occasions I happened to break stories concerning him and factions in the local Labour Party. He attempted both times to get the then Press

The adoption meeting of Mr Eddie Milne, Labour Candidate for Blyth, took place on 26th September 1964. He is seen here (centre) as the voting figures are being read out by a regional official watched by Wilf Holliday, the Labour agent.

Council to discipline me but on both occasions the complaints were rejected.

By now Eddie had moved from the Labour Rooms and constituency office claiming he could not trust the officials there and was working from a company's premises managed by a fellow Scot, Angus Galloway. It was to this office in Carlton Street I was invited for a 'clear the air' chat by Eddie following his first unsuccessful application to the Press Council. This was over a front page lead story I did in the *Sunday Sun* concerning a report compiled by the MP criticising the local party on its handling of the what turned out to be a highly successful election campaign.

Local journalists build up contacts and it so happened I had a number in the local party and also serving on the Blyth Borough Council. Obviously the factions within the party were prepared to pass on tit-bits which showed their opponents in a bad light. Now it was these 'leaks' and particularly those involving him that were getting under the skin of Eddie and I was tipped off he was determined to find out who was passing the information to me.

I arrived at the meeting to find Eddie sitting behind his desk with Angus Galloway alongside him. I immediately sensed Eddie had Angus there as a witness to any hint I might give. The meeting lasted shorter than Eddie had intended after I told him I knew whom he suspected as the leak and that I would swear out an affidavit at my solicitors saying that person was not the one. Eddie was way, way off the mark in believing it was Wilf Holliday – he was not my main source. Indeed he was the most loyal of Socialists. Anyhow he shook my hand and said he hoped we could make a fresh start.

The next day I was tipped off about an apparent row brewing between the MP and the women's section of the party. The ladies claimed Eddie had insulted their officials, I doorstepped, that is waited outside the meeting, in the Labour Rooms. The first one out was Peter Mortakis, a local councillor and up till then a staunch Milneite. 'I'm not telling you anything,' he shouted at me as he passed by, 'you're just out to get Eddie.' The story duly appeared as the main lead in the *Sunday Sun* and the Press Council again rejected a complaint.

Within a couple of months Peter Mortakis was also lined up against Eddie Milne after a falling out. While my main source of information is now dead I do not think it right to reveal him as members of his immediate family still live in the town. But what I can say is that MI5 had nothing on my source. A cryptic telephone call to my office would see me head for a nearby back lane. A figure would walk down the lane towards me and, as he passed, documents or notes would be handed over without a word being said. I rather think he enjoyed the cloak and dagger aspect.

In those 1960s days the minutes of Blyth Borough Council were not issued to the press until the actual night of the meeting in the Seaforth Street Council Chamber making it impossible to run any stories beforehand. Somehow or other I always managed to have a copy as soon as they were issued to members and was able to take my pick of the stories for publication before the actual meeting.

One thing can be said about Blyth Council is that their monthly meetings were never shorter than those of Newbiggin Urban Council. Once a month I had to drive to the town for the meeting and you had to be dead on time. I arrived ninety seconds late on one occasion to find the meeting over. A 100% Labour Council had already made decisions at the group meeting and the rubber stamping of, and the length of the meeting, was decided by how long it took to move and second the entire set of minutes!

It was rather ironic when Blyth Council launched its regular hunt for the person or persons responsible for the leaking of information to the Press. It was actually led by my own 'Deep Throat'!

Jackie Milburn

My dad and I often watched 'Wor' Jack in action at St James' Park and it was with some pride I came to know him as a friend in later years. In 1965 I was working for the *Sunday Mirror* in Manchester and the sports editor got me a press box ticket for the visit of Newcastle United to Old Trafford. I discovered the North East press corps were at a nearby hotel and after work on the Friday night popped round to see them. Jack, who was working for a national Sunday paper, and I got into conversation. He was not staying at that hotel, he said, as he could not afford it but was in a smaller bed breakfast establishment. I was shocked to learn he was forced to do this because he was on a flat £25 a week from which he had to pay his own transport and hotel costs when travelling to away games. At that time I was on £35 a week with my weekly expenses way in excess of that.

His salary was something I remembered when I returned to the North East the following year to rejoin the *Journal*. Peter Kane was the editor of the *Sunday Sun* and I let him know, to his delight, that Jackie might be interested in

The great Jackie Milburn in action.

joining his staff if the money was right. When I phoned Jack he readily agreed to come into Thomson House for a chat with Peter and when he left he told me he was on his way to hand in his notice at the Sunday national. He had accepted Peter's offer of £35 a week plus a minimum of £20 a week expenses. Jack later rang Peter and me to apologise and say the national's sports editor had more than matched the offer and he had decided to stay with them.

Later, when at Radio Newcastle, I arranged for Jack to come into our record library at Broadcasting Centre on a Saturday where he spent the morning dubbing off the latest tracks of his favourite music – country and western.

We sat next to each other in the temporary press box at St James' Park when the West Stand was being renovated. By then, although he kept it quiet, Jack was suffering from cancer and at times it was a struggle for him to write his report. On occasions I used to help and to save him having to walk around the park to the press conference after the game I provided him with the quotes he needed.

The last time I saw Jack was at St James' but he felt so ill he returned home before the kick-off after arranging for the match to be covered by a freelance. I must say I shed many tears when attending his funeral service in Newcastle Cathedral and again when I saw the thousands lining the streets of Newcastle in a final tribute to him.

The Callers Pegasus matches featuring international cricket sides at Jesmond in Newcastle were also a great social occasion with receptions being held at Linden Hall. Here the author is pictured with the former international fast bowler, Frank Tyson, and 'Wor Jackie'.

Sporting Occasions

On taking early retirement from BBC Radio Newcastle the one thing I did not miss was the constant looking at your watch as your on-air deadline approached, Being sports producer meant you were at the whim of your interviewees, particularly soccer managers on a Friday. The most notorious of these were Bill McGarry and Laurie McMenemy. On one occasion McGarry kept me waiting from 9.30 until half past 12, despite two interventions on my behalf by Joe Harvey, for our weekly appointment and then had the nerve to ask me how I was when I entered his office at St James' Park. He was not pleased when I told him exactly what I thought. I got my interview and dashed back to Broadcasting Centre, fortunately just up Barrack Road, in time for my five past one sports bulletin. I may say after my outburst Bill always saw me at the appointed time.

Laurie did not keep me sitting on the carpeted steps outside his office in Roker Park for that length of time but an hour and a bit was not uncommon. The Big Man always gave me the impression of being unsure of himself and regularly after our interview would unburden his problems to me off the record.

He rose in my estimation when I put it to Jack Charlton, then boss of Newcastle, and to Laurie that I would like them to do a show entitled 'Big Jack and Big Mac'. It would last half an hour and would be recorded and go out on a Saturday lunchtime. There was money involved, I told them. The fee was £350 each but Laurie said he would do it if the station used the cash to buy season tickets for Roker Park for pensioners. The pensioners got their season tickets but the listeners did not get the two managers. Two weeks before the programme was

A charity match featuring Radio Newcastle against the East Enders was held at the Gateshead International Stadium. Jackie Milburn managed the Newcastle team and is seen here with the author, Nick Berry and Tom Watts.

due to be aired Jack quit Newcastle after his family were verbally abused by fans during a pre-season friendly at St James' Park. The programme became the 'Big Mac Show'.

A lasting memory of Jack Charlton was when I learned his 50th birthday was coming up just a few days before mine. Now Jack was notorious for his meanness as far as cigarettes were concerned, in fact he was reputed to have cadged smokes from pensioners standing watching the players training. On this occasion I bought a packet of twenty Benson and Hedges and took them with me one Friday to our weekly interview at the Benwell training ground. I wished him a happy birthday and pulled the packet out. I had hardly got them six inches from my pocket when, in a fraction of a second, Jack had them out of my hand and secreted in his jacket.

A couple of years after I left Radio Newcastle I invited Jack to speak in aid of Blyth Spartans at a dinner in the clubhouse and he was a wow. Although he told me not to reveal it at the time, he came for a vastly reduced fee.

The one thing I like about Big Jack is that what you see is what you get – as the Irish later found out.

Lawrie McMenemy's sudden resignation from Sunderland, while not totally expected as the side was heading for relegation, came so suddenly it caught the North East media by surprise. I was hauled out of bed to chase the story. Laurie though had flown the coop. His neighbours in Washington said he had left the previous night so I headed for Roker Park to join the press hordes outside the main entrance. I was in the radio car and occasionally was called upon to broadcast what had happened and what was happening. Our presenter asked me who I thought would be next in the job. I replied that I would not be surprised to see Bob Murray roll up in his limousine accompanied by Bob Stokoe, a man he greatly admired and felt should not have left the club when he did. Five minutes later his car arrived and Bob Murray headed straight for me. 'You were spot on,' he said with a grin, as Bob Stokoe got out of the car to join him. They had been listening to Radio Newcastle on the journey.

This picture of me (complete with top piece) and Ian Botham was taken by BBC photographer George Pope who blew it up very large. In a competition among colleagues for an appropriate caption it appeared on the newsroom board with a bubble from Ian's mouth saying: 'You see Jim, mine doesn't come off!'

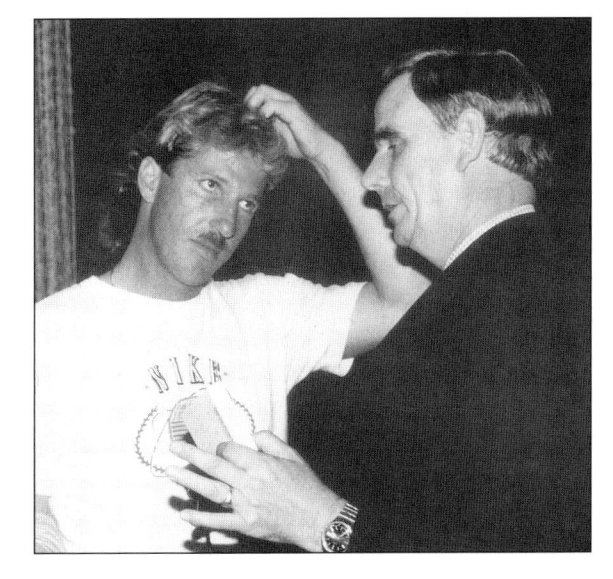

The Boys in Black and White

A sports producer on a BBC local radio station is usually a one man operation, except on a Saturday when he brings in his team of part-timers for the five-hour long afternoon epic. He is also on a 24 hours a day stand-by being at the beck and call of colleagues. So it was when the phone rang just after six that morning with the news producer informing me that the Sun had an exclusive about Paul Gasgoine signing for Tottenham Hotspur. Could I come in and talk about the Newcastle United star. Within half an hour I was on the air pontificating about Gazza and after I had done my duty it was off on the hunt for the vanished England midfielder. When a trip to his Whickham home failed to yield him it was back to the office to continue the search by telephone. Now BBC Radio Newcastle had by this time moved into the brand new Pink Palace – North East Television Centre – and shared a newsroom with their TV colleagues.

It was while I was hunting the elusive star I recalled my first face to face meeting with him. I had seen him on the pitch turning out for the juniors and the reserves and met him at the Benwell training ground headquarters, a wooden hut actually. He was cleaning the boots of a certain Kevin Keegan. Even then his personality and confidence shone through and he was universally liked even if he was forever asking to be interviewed on TV or radio.

As his stature grew so did his cockiness. On one occasion, when an established first teamer, he tried to cross verbal swords with the much respected Sunday newspaper journalist Tony Hardisty and lost. As a result several members of the Press, sheltering inside the building, and one innocent radio journalist, were ordered out by Glenn Roeder, his mentor, on the instructions of the then manager Willie McFaul. Fortunately a couple of weeks later we were re-admitted.

On one occasion he borrowed my tape recorder ostensibly to help him teach United's new Brazilian striker Mirandinha to speak Geordie. The phrase he taught the innocent South American was so obscene it had to be wiped, but only after it had been played to male colleagues in the office. That was the second time a soccer star had borrowed my machine. The first was when Kevin Keegan, encouraged by Terry McDermott, interviewed the boss, Arthur Cox, at St James' Park about team tactics. It was hilarious and ended with Arthur tongue-tied and the two reprobates doubled up with laughter.

Arthur was a likeable personality even if on a few occasions I thought some of his actions were rather weird. The weekly interviews always took place at Benwell after training and on a number of occasions Arthur was drying himself off after a shower when answering the questions. Another time we were about to start the interview when there came a knock on the door and a junior player came in carrying his mug of tea. 'Get out,' Arthur roared. 'The last time you brought my tea we lost. Get someone else to bring it in.' The youngster suitably chastened, did as he was told. My tape recorder had to be in the same spot on his desk and I always had to stand on the right and he on the left. Possibly the weirdest came after a fan sent 12 good luck chains and Arthur got his number two, Willie McFaul, to distribute them to the team he had selected. But back to the hunt for Gazza.

The first team was not due to train that day but a gut feeling got me to drive up to the Benwell training ground and sure enough there was Gazza with his friend and team-mate Brian Tinnion. Both were sitting in Gazza's brand new car – bought no doubt, with the handsome payment for the *Sun* exclusive. Gazza was not too keen on an interview but thanks to the intervention of Brian he agreed and it was conducted with me kneeling by the driver's door with Gazza remaining in the car. After the chat I told the star that Steve Sutton, my oppo in BBC television in Newcastle, was interested in having an interview with him and asked him where he was heading. Gazza said he would be at St James' Park for the next hour but I had better tell Steve that the

As Sports Producer of Radio Newcastle the author was called upon to present Kevin Keegan with a pit lamp on the occasion of his retirement as a player. Kevin's grandfather was a Durham miner. Kevin, of course, later returned as manager of Newcastle and the acquaintance was renewed.

interview would cost him. 'How much?' I said.

'£10,000,' came the reply. And after my laughter subsided I realised he was serious. Funny how media money can corrupt.

On my return to the Pink Palace, Steve came across to find out if I had been successful in my hunt for Gazza. On hearing I had and that Gazza would be at St James' Park said, 'Great, I'll get a film crew together.'

'Hang on,' I replied. 'It's going to cost you.'

'How much?" asked Steve. I told him. After he'd recovered from the shock he set off to have a chat with the player – minus the film crew. Ten minutes later he arrived back from St James' Park rather ashen faced.

'Was he there?" I asked.

'Yes,' replied Steve.

'So, did he ask for £10,000?'

'No,' said Steve. 'He said because it was me it would only be £5,000.' Needless to say the camera crew did not visit St James' that day.

The Unsung Heroes

I made many friends while at Radio Newcastle with Stan Long, the Gateshead athletics coach, who trained Brendan Foster, one of them. In the early 1980s I suggested to Stan, who worked for the Gateshead Sport and Recreation Department then headed by Brendan, about the possibility of a half marathon run between Newcastle and Sunderland. 'The Bridges Race' would start on the Tyne Bridge and finish at the Wearmouth Bridge. Stan was all for it and said it could be organised. I told him I would take up the possibility of sponsorship with Geoff Talbot, the manager of Radio Newcastle. Geoff said he would consider it and over the next six weeks, following reminders by Stan, I made two more approaches to Geoff. He eventually declined to back the race. The next year the Great North Run came into being.

Radio Newcastle was given permission to broadcast the second Great North Run with our radio car at the front of the race, The 'car' was actually a van with an up and over rear door. Stan Long and I sat on the floor in the back with our legs dangling towards the road. The race-timing car was the only vehicle between the top athletes and us when the race got underway. We congratulated ourselves as we crossed the Tyne Bridge on having such a prime position. Unfortunately for us Mike McLeod, the Elswick Harrier, decided to run away from the other athletes and Stan and I found ourselves looking only at him with the rest literally out of sight. Fortunately Stan is a good talker with a fund of athletic knowledge and kept it going until Mike crossed the line. Despite our limited view the broadcast appeared to go down well.

What did not go down well was when I was the announcer for the Junior Great North Run, which has become an integral part of the Great North weekend being held the day before the major event. Brendan and his colleague John Caine had left the employ of Gateshead Council some years earlier and joined Nike as their UK top brass. The two parted company with the American firm on less than cordial terms and went into the sports promotion business with Nova International and later launched their own sportswear company View From.

On the occasion of this Junior Great North Run, which was run inside and outside Gateshead Stadium, Nike, who were not the race sponsors, handed out hundreds of cardboard eye shades to the competitors all bearing their Nike slogan. In addition they had taken over the forecourt of a garage outside the stadium where they had a huge inflatable advertising their products. This did not go down well at all with the two former employees as the television cameras could not avoid getting the motif in shot. The message was sent up to me on the bridge overlooking the course to make an announcement telling the runners to take the shades off. It was an impossible task as hundreds of them were being worn. I declined to do so.

I was not invited to be the announcer the following year.

An international athletics match at Gateshead Stadium almost gave me a heart attack. It was a triangular tournament involving a team from Ethiopia and Stan asked me if I could get a copy of the Ethiopian national anthem for the opening ceremony of the games. I contacted

The author was the first radio journalist to interview Steve Cram. He was a seventeen-year-old at Hebburn High School and about to make his name in the Emsley Carr Invitation Mile in London. Subsequently the author became very friendly with his coach, Jimmy Hedley, and his parents, Bill and Mia Cram, and attended Steve's engagement party and later produced an outside broadcast of his wedding in Jarrow.

our record library in Broadcasting House, London, and eventually they said they had a copy but were not sure how relevant it was to the current regime. It was sent 'up the line' to us at Newcastle where it was recorded and I took the tape to Stan at the stadium the day before the match. He was sitting in the stand watching the Ethiopians train and my farewell words to him were to let the team manager hear the tape to make sure it was the correct one. The next day, all hell broke loose when the Ethiopians walked off the track and said they would not perform as they had been insulted. The anthem I had provided was the one played when the country had an emperor and not the current piece introduced after the republican take-over of the country. It took tremendous tact and diplomacy by Brendan Foster and his team to persuade the Ethiopians to return to the track. Although not named in newspaper reports I was blamed for the cock-up.

I stand by my version.

Stan, who was a regular contributor to my Friday night sports show, is one of the unsung heroes of sport. He has devoted countless thousands of hours to training youngsters and even now on a Thursday night his home in Low Fell is a meeting place for of a group of young runners. After training they are regally entertained to refreshments provided by Stan's wife, Joan. I remember some years ago writing to 10 Downing Street proposing Jimmy Hedley for an award for training two athletes who had won world titles, Steve Cram and David Sharpe. I also proposed Stan for his unstinting work for athletics.

They still don't have letters after their names. Shame.

The Mighty Spartans

Television proved an interesting and demanding occupation but was also a frustrating one. You could work on a story all day, watch it on the screen for ninety seconds, then it would be gone forever. At least in newspapers you could always keep your cuttings. During my two years on *Look North* writing for Mike Neville there were highs and lows. One high was when Blyth Spartans reached the fifth round of the FA Cup in the late 1970s. They were due to travel to Wrexham on the Friday before the match and I suggested to the *Look North* editor, John Bird, we got the team coach to stop at Broadcasting House, which was then in New Bridge Street, and give them a champagne send off. He agreed and I contacted Jim Turney, the chairman of the Spartans and secretary, George Watson, who were both all for the idea and arranged for the arrival to coincide with the time the programme was broadcast. The only problem was in those days we did not have portable cameras.

To broadcast live meant carrying one of the three extremely heavy, early models normally kept permanently in the first floor studio, down the stairs and out on to the path at the front of the building. This was achieved with a struggle by four strong men and the cables were then run back up the path and the stairs and connected up in the studio. It was then we realised the door of the coach was on the side away from the camera because of the one-way system in operation in New Bridge Street. In addition there was ice and snow on the pavement in front of Broadcasting House, which posed a risk to the limbs of the players. Newcastle City Council sent down their snow clearing team and the police halted traffic to allow the coach to be driven against the normal flow. This meant we got the players and officials alighting from the bus in camera shot. A merry party then ensued with live interviews being conducted and the team toasted by Mike, Stuart Prebble, Fiona Johnston and the rest of the *Look North* crew.

I wondered at the, time if Jacky Marks, the team coach, was taking a stock of his 'speed oil' down to Wales with him. Jack always insisted on the players having a swig of his magic elixir before a match. 'Speed oil' was actually whisky and it certainly seemed to work the charm that season.

The charm failed, however, to stop the corner flag falling over which led to Wrexham's equalising goal and subsequent defeat in the replay. A defeat which stopped the Spartans entertaining Arsenal in the sixth round at Roker Park. Anyhow the send off proved tremendously successful.

Blyth Spartans famous cup run brought the town alive. Listening to the cup draw must have provided Radio Two with their biggest ever audience in East Northumberland. Here from left to right waiting for the draw are the leading lights of the Spartans: Jim Turney (chairman), Terry Johnson, (striker) Brian Slane, Dave Clarke (goalkeeper), George Watson (secretary), John Donohoe (vice chairman) and John Waterson (captain).

Terry Johnson nets for the Spartans in the fifth round tie against Wrexham at the Racecourse Ground in the match which featured the infamous corner flag falling down incident which led to the Welsh side's equaliser.

The cover of the record produced to celebrate the Spartans' memorable cup run.

Clangers At The Beeb

Another incident, which stands out in my mind, is when the *Look North* programme was almost completely ruined. I had been busy all day on my news. It was to be read by Tom Kilgour and was due to last seven minutes and include film clips. On national television the 'and finally' story is something quite light-hearted and entertaining. So it was in regional television. You sought to have a nice 'and finally' at the end of your news bulletin. On this occasion I had a lovely story with a 35 seconds of super film showing a duckling which had been adopted by a cat. Thirty-five seconds of film meant 140 words and, if I say so myself, I excelled myself with the prose. In those days, particularly in the regions, there were no video cameras with everything being shot on film with the sound on a separate tape. This meant all the film inserts for the programme had to be edited together on one large reel, the sound being laced on to another reel and the engineer making sure they were in sync. On one occasion the reels were mixed up and when the film was cued all that went out was black. The sound tape was on the vision machine.

We had a Geordie film editor named Geoff Wonfor who was an ardent Newcastle United supporter with a tremendous interest in pop music. He loved editing items on soccer and music but lacked, as he

Stuart Prebble in the foreground, later to achieve fame and lose his job as head of failed ITV Digital, was a reporter on BBC's Look North when Blyth Spartans called in at Broadcasting House on the way to their FA Cup Fifth Round tie at Wrexham. Alongside him, also in Spartans colours, is reporter Fiona Johnston while centre stage is taken by Mike Neville with players and officials of the Blyth side. To Mike's right is coach Jacky Marks.

would no doubt admit, much enthusiasm for anything else. On this particular day he had been rather lax in editing a non-music or sport piece which resulted in him running very late. His was the final film to be added to the large spool, which already contained all the inserts for the programme including my news clips. He managed it with only a couple of minutes to go to the start of the programme.

It was while he was rushing it in his arms downstairs to the production room he slipped and the spool went flying, unravelling all the way down the passage to the front door. There was no time to restore the film, Mike did his usual magnificent ad-lib job while Tom Kilgour was instructed to read the news section at the top of the programme instead of later. And so it was that viewers were regaled with seven minutes of news without pictures and no doubt were extremely puzzled when Tom read, very straight-faced, my little tale about the duck and the cat! Me, I was stunned to see my day's work ruined.

At the news desk I had the authority to hire freelance cameramen to provide me with film. On one occasion a story was filed from Darlington about how the owner of an Alsatian guard dog had got off a charge of keeping a dangerous animal. The magistrates ruled the person who had been attacked had been trespassing and come too close to the dog, which was on a chain. I asked the cameraman, Gary Price, for a shot of the dog on the premises where he was kept to go with the story. Three hours later I was still waiting. Eventually Gary rang in.

The medieval banquets at Delaval Hall, now unfortunately discontinued, were extremely popular in the 1970s and '80s. The visit of a team from the Atlanta TV station which acted as host to the BBC earlier in the year led to a visit to the Seaton Delaval venue. Rod Taylor, the American reporter was made king for the night. Also in the picture are: Steve Byerly, the American cameraman (front row left) Bill Midgely (back row left) who ran the banquets and also acted as Mine Host and John Bird (back row right) the BBC Look North editor.

'Where the hell are you?' I asked.

'In hospital,' came the reply.

'What on earth for?'

'I got too close to the dog.'

He was off work for ten days.

It was after I joined the staff of Radio Newcastle as sports and light entertainment producer I had the chance of a trip to Atlanta with the Friendship Force. I was to link up again with Mike to produce an hour-long radio piece entitled 'Mike in Georgia'. Mike was also to front some television pieces from Georgia for *Look North*. Mike and I stayed a week with Steve Byerly, a cameraman with an Atlanta TV station and his wife, and then for the second week with a local doctor and his wife. My programme compared industry, education, radio and politics in Georgia with the North East. During the course of making the programme we got to meet Ted Turner, the man who launched CNN and later married and divorced Jane Fonda, and Newt Gingridge, who was to become the powerful leader of the United States Congress. Mike interviewed Newt, who was seeking re-election to Congress, at a political breakfast in Atlanta. It was a fascinating event attended by hundreds of supporters.

The following year I made two trips abroad on behalf of the BBC. The first was to Australia to cover the Commonwealth Games in Brisbane for the entire BBC local radio chain and the second was to the New York marathon where I followed the fortunes of North East runners, including television personality Bill Steel.

Bill and I roomed together in New York and learned very quickly you did not stray too far from your hotel at night. On a walk we were so immersed in conversation we did not notice we had strayed into a black area. The looks we were getting from groups hanging around led us to pretty quickly head back to the bright lights of Broadway. It was while out for another walk we spotted Rudolf Nureyev in a bookshop studying a tome on furniture of the middle ages and around the corner Anthony Quinn alighted from a taxi and entered a rather swish apartment block. We did not visit a Broadway show – the lowest ticket price being £48 but both have since regretted not investing £45 each on a helicopter ride around Manhattan.

The author was chosen to cover the New York Marathon for BBC World Service, Radio Newcastle and Radio Cleveland in l982. He is pictured here at the start of the race which finished in Central Park.

Darts On The Radio

Local radio can be a most fulfilling and an interesting one at times, particularly when the winter weather hits the soccer programme and you have four hours to fill.

On one occasion when all the games we were due to cover had fallen by the wayside I decided on a radio first – darts.

We had the newly crowned world master's champion living on Tyneside and I rang him up and asked if he would come into the studio at Crestina House in Archbold Terrace, Jesmond, and take on all-comers. We then appealed to our listeners for any would-be challengers and were inundated with replies.

Now even loyal members of my Saturday afternoon team queried having darts on radio. But as I pointed out to them tennis matches had been broadcast for many years relying on the commentators and sounds. We rigged up a board in Studio Two complete with sound effects mike, a commentator with a lip mike and a reporter to interview the challengers before they played.

The only thing wrong was that the first three challengers beat the world champion. During a break I asked him what was wrong. He replied that he only played well after he had been drinking Newcastle Brown Ale. I immediately sent out to the Archer pub, opposite the studio, and imported a crate of brown ale.

The champion was right. After a couple of pints he won the rest of the challenges easily.

I came in for some ironic skit from national and local radio sporting colleagues up and down the country but was in the great position of being able to challenge a national radio station which announced a 'first' some years later – darts on the radio.

I have to admit, though, it has not really caught on.

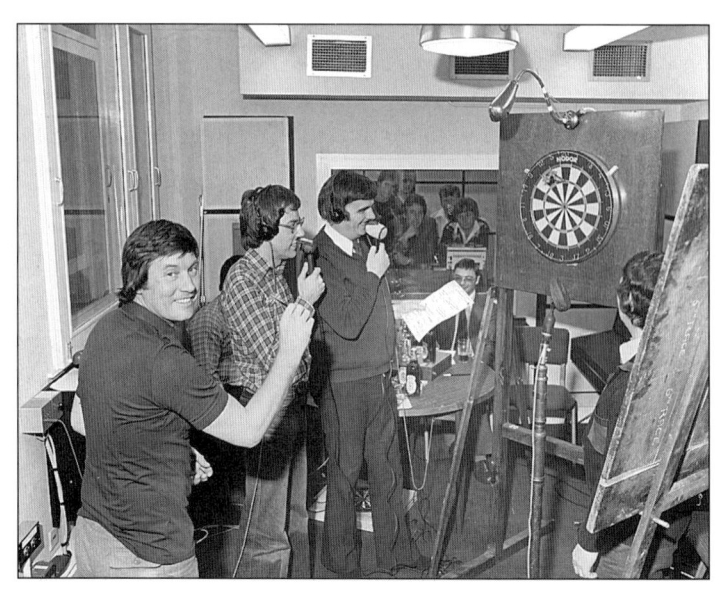

Radio Newcastle scored a first with darts on radio one Saturday afternoon when the weather had wiped out the entire sporting programme. Ron Mellowes of Newcastle had become a national champion at the sport and took on all-comers in Studio Two at Crestina House in Jesmond. From left to right: the champion, Railton Howes and the author.

Media Moguls

A career in journalism brings you into contact with many people, some of whom go on to bigger things. Greg Dyke, the current Director General of the BBC, was a colleague of mine in the early 1970s at the head office of the *Journal* in Newcastle. He was a very amiable chap with a quick-fire delivery of speech which, with his South London accent, made understanding a little difficult on occasions, I was deputy news editor and Greg was one of a team of reporters under my control. As Christmas approached I suggested we do a pantomime in our newsroom at Thomson House in aid of the National Union of Journalists Widows and Orphans Fund. The requisite permission was obtained from the management and Phil Penfold, arts and entertainments editor for our sister paper the *Evening Chronicle*, was called in to write the script, while I directed and used the red pencil of the more obscene lines Phil had written. The cast was selected from colleagues and Greg Dyke accepted the part of the Major Domo with the current *Journal* columnist, Avril Deane, as Dandini. The stage on which we were to perform was made from a number of reporters' desks pushed together. Rehearsals were hilarious and the two performances of the panto, watched by virtually the entire staff in the building, went off triumphantly.

It was some weeks later Greg came to me and said, 'I'm not cut out to be a reporter.' He was, he said, leaving to work in social services with a council in London. The next I heard of him was when he introduced Roland Rat to the foundering *Good Morning* TV programme. The rat saved the show and led to Greg eventually becoming a millionaire when he took up his share options on the sale of the company producing the programme.

The departure of Greg to London meant he could not appear in the second pantomime staged by editorial staff in Thomson House. It was Little Red Riding Hood and starred Piers Merchant, then a reporter, but later to become a Conservative MP who was exposed by a Sunday

The Thomson House editorial pantomime, with reporters' desks as the stage proved highly popular in the early 1970s. Appearing in the first was Greg Dyke (centre with beard), the current director general of the BBC who was a reporter on the Journal at the time.

newspaper for having a rather stormy extra marital affair. It led to his losing his seat in the House of Commons. Also in the cast were Peter Mortimer, one of the North East's leading poets, and Avril Deane, the Journal columnist.

While Greg Dyke is now exercising great power at the BBC another former colleague has lost all the power he had. Stuart Prebble quit ITV when the digital service he was heading collapsed because of the Football League financial commitments. Stuart was a student at Newcastle University and after gaining his degree joined the BBC *Look North* team as a reporter. At that time I was the regional journalist responsible for getting out the news section of the programme.

Stuart eventually moved on in the BBC and then joined independent television where he produced *World in Action* for a time before moving up the managerial ladder with Granada.

An international personality now, who started his journalistic career in Blyth, is Robert Fisk, the Middle East correspondent of the Independent on Sunday who was formerly with the Sunday Times.

I was chief reporter of the 'Curve' area which took in Morpeth, Ashington and Blyth and Bob joined me at my office in Seaforth Street from where we served all three papers, the *Journal, Evening Chronicle*

In 1982 the author was named Radio Sports Broadcasting Personality of the Year in the North East and received a silver salver from the then Minister for Sport, Mr Neil McFarlane, at the Northern Sports Foundation dinner in Newcastle Civic Centre. He is seen here at the dinner with Bob Wrack, the BBC Radio Newcastle station manager, and David McCreery, the Newcastle United midfielder.

and *Sunday Sun*. He was an 18 year old straight out of taking his 'A' levels at grammar school and had failed to obtain a university place in the south of England.

He proved to be a very willing trainee and it was obvious from the off he was going to succeed as a journalist. Robert had digs in Middleton Street and recently returned to the area while he was researching an article on the changing face of journalism. It was only by reading the article I realised how cold and starving he was when in Blyth. On one occasion he missed a stabbing story because he was sitting huddled over a brazier at the Harbour gates talking to the watchman. Fortunately I saw a news flash of the stabbing on the late Tyne Tees news and was able to file a story to the *Journal*.

Bob is the double of Woody Allen, even more so as he has grown older. He made his name with his reports for *The Times* in Northern Ireland, a series from Beirut during the terrible conflict there and is continuing to win plaudits for his articles and stories from the Middle East over the Israeli and Palestinian situation. It is with some pride I take a little share of Bob's spotlight.

Newcastle United Radio Magpie

Sir John Hall is a very decisive man who, when he sets his mind to it, gets what he wants. And Sir John wanted a radio station for Newcastle United. He had seen Manchester United's at Old Trafford and he gave out the instructions for one to come into operation as Radio Magpie broadcasting from St James' Park. The necessary one-day licence for broadcasting on home match days was duly obtained by a rather dubious Freddie Fletcher, the chief executive. A 20 foot high mast was erected just inside the entrance gates to the park and an advert was placed for a presenter-producer. A former Radio Newcastle presenter, John Oley, was appointed. It was a surprising choice as John, a pleasant and talented disc jockey, had never had any interest in soccer. He, in turn, invited Evan Martin, one of my former reporters at Radio Newcastle, and myself to join the team. Advertising, it was expected, would fund the station. It was an expectation, which never had a chance of being fulfilled. Radio Magpie was launched two months into the 1994-95 season with a limited five-mile broadcasting range but advertisers just did not want to know when our part-time sales girl contacted them.

The haphazard range of our broadcasts caused no end of bother with some people eight miles away being able to listen but others much closer not being able to get a signal. In addition nobody told Kevin Keegan and his players that the station was to broadcast and accordingly no provision had been made for them to be made available for interview. This led to John and I having a meeting with Kevin when approval was given for Radio Magpie to have priority access to the playing staff. Kevin also agreed to be interviewed in the players tunnel immediately after the final whistle which would really give the station a scoop. A disaster, as it turned out.

Being the roving reporter for Radio Magpie meant I was really behind the scenes. We went on the air at ten o'clock and I was able to watch and report fitness tests being carried out on players on the morning of the match. In addition I had access to the referee, the groundsman and the ticket office manager. I also got an insight into Kevin Keegan's thinking. On one occasion I was standing on the touchline when Kevin and Terry McDermott gave instructions to the groundsman to turn on the sprinkler system. There was only four hours to kick-off time but Kevin wanted a wet top surface to allow the ball to skid along the turf.

Radio Magpie did not get off to the best of starts with Kevin. We began broadcasting on the Saturday Manchester United visited St James' Park. True to his word Kevin came straight up to me in the tunnel at the end of the game to give the first post-match interview. The trouble was John, our presenter, was busily engaged in banter on the game with Evan, who had been commentating, and did not have his two way radio on, my only means of communication with him. Give Kevin his due he stood with me for five minutes while I attempted to get him on the air but eventually he walked off in disgust.

At the outset Kevin was a hail fellow-well-met with a quip and a joke, particularly about my battered trilby, whenever we met on match days. It was noticeable as the season progressed how the pressure was getting to him. The banter was gone and he was becoming a little on the quick-tempered side, particularly with the media, Radio Magpie included.

Tony Blair was a VIP visitor to St James' Park at one home game and I asked Sir John Hall if he could persuade the Leader of the Opposition to come on air. The request was successful and the interview took place in the players' tunnel. After the usual introductory banter I asked Mr Blair, a professed Newcastle United supporter, if he was a Gallowgate or Leazes ender. I knew by his face he did not have a clue as to what I was talking about and I rapidly moved on to another subject.

Sir John regularly popped into the Radio Magpie studio, which was a very tiny room alongside the Sky Television box and overlooked the Leazes End goal. He seemed very keen but Radio Magpie created no impact on the staff at St James' Park. They preferred to listen to Radio Two on the internal system on matchdays despite a couple of approaches that it be tuned to us. During the seven months I was involved with Radio Magpie we had heard rumours that Freddie Fletcher was seeking Metro Radio to take over the running of the station to facilitate advertising income. And so it happened. Metro moved in the following season and after a couple of years Radio Magpie ceased to exist.

SECTION EIGHT

SPORT

The Blyth schools side in the 1935-36 season boasted a young goalkeeper who was destined to play in the Football League for Huddersfield Town. Harry Mills (back centre) was spotted when playing for Blyth Spartans. On his retirement from playing he returned to Blyth where he died in 1999. Also on the picture (the boy with his hands on his hips) is Bill Emery, who was an excellent all-round sportsman being a top snooker player, golfer and captain of Blyth cricket team. The young player wearing his Northumberland cap is Stan Riddell who also showed his prowess as a fast bowler with Blyth Phoenix cricket club. R.W. Robertson (extreme right middle row) is the father of Peter Robertson, Blyth fast bowler, singer and piano accompanist to the Blyth and Beaconsfield operatic societies Back row: J. Pearson (Secretary of Blyth Schools FA), J. Hooper, B. Coulson, H.O. Mills, W. (Danny) Dawson (Chairman of Blyth Schools FA), W. Emery. Middle row: Ald T.C. Blackburn (President), W. Milburn, T. Downie, R.S. Wilson, R.R. Walton, F. Mitchell and R.W. Robertson. Front row: G. Hudson, J.F. Hertwick, F.W. Chapple, Coun J.W. Heatley (Mayor of Blyth), S.S. Riddell, Ald J.J. Reilly, N. Brannigan, J. Thompson and D. Lake.

Cricketing Tales

Jim Harland skippered the Princess Louise Modern School cricket team and later played 'friendly' cricket for Blyth Phoenix before graduating to Blyth third team and subsequently the first team which played in the old Northumberland League.

Although brought into the first team as a replacement fast bowler when George Robinson retired after many years service, Jim ended up as a opening bat and change bowler. He scored an unbeaten maiden century against Backworth and had best bowling figures of 6-38 against County Club.

He eventually skippered the first team for three seasons and although still playing was appointed chairman of the club and organised many fund-raising events including a donkey derby, indoor barbecue, baby show and big beat ball.

In the 1978 and 1979 seasons Jim turned out for Boldon in the Durham Senior League and won the batting trophy on both occasions. He returned to Blyth and finished his playing career in the second team taking eight wickets for six against Morpeth to get the side promoted to the B1 section of the Northumberland League.

Blyth First XI take the field at Benwell Hill in a Northumberland League match in May 1966. From left to right: Steve Grey, Cecil Pearson, Melvin Bruce, Ian Darling, Pat Hughes, the author, Ron Atkinson, Brian Storey, Neil Mitcheson, Frank Scott and Peter Robertson.

In Play Or Not In Play

The day of the semi-final dawned mild and overcast in August 1958. As an alleged fast bowler with the longest run in the league I stretched my six foot two inch frame and contemplated an extra hour's lie in with relish. I would need all my strength for the coming battle on the concrete cricket wicket laid in the middle of the Broadway Field next to the Blyth Spartans soccer ground. The Town Boys' Club against the North Blyth British Rail Staff Association was a tie that had the whole of the Blyth Tradesmen's League buzzing. The rivalry between the two clubs took in not only cricket but also soccer, billiards and snooker.

The smell of bacon frying downstairs tempted me to leave the comfort of my bed but no, rest came first. With luck, my mother might offer me breakfast in bed. Fat chance. No table, no food, was the cardinal rule of the household, I turned over and let my thoughts drift to the match due to start that Sunday afternoon at half past two. Thirty-five overs a side and to the winners a run-out in the final on the hallowed turf of Blyth Cricket Club of the Northumberland League. I had never played on the Plessey Road Ground but that would change if we won the semi-final.

Blyth had declined to put a team in the Midweek Tradesmen's League claiming they did not have the time but everyone knew it was snobbishness. They had, however, agreed reluctantly to a request to let the league cup final be played there on the edge of the square. And so my team, the Boys' Club, was only one game away from 'Lords'. The North Blyth were skippered by Ralph Dempster, one of the leagues characters. He was the only wicketkeeper in the league who did not wear a protective box. Ralphy hinted that it restricted his movements behind the stumps but never really explained why.

A knock on the bedroom door woke me from my musings and mother entered with a pot of tea in one hand and a thick bacon sandwich on a plate in the other. 'Get to the final and it'll be egg and bacon,' she said after placing the welcoming sight on the bedside table. The remark surprised me as Mum had never shown any interest in sport. I murmured my thanks through a mouthful of bread and bacon. I instantly decided it would be the last food I would have until after the semi-final. No roast beef and Yorkshire pudding for me at lunchtime. I would have a fry up later.

It was after noon when I decided to leave my bed to prepare for the big match. A quick wash and a shave was followed by the donning of a white shirt, old but clean, grey flannels, a double helping of socks and a pair of white plimsolls. There was no luxury of a pavilion in the Tradesmen's League. A casual stroll down to Broadway Field got me there in time to see the concrete track being covered with matting. The Tradesmen's League expected teams to provide an umpire each and cup semi-finals were no exception. Dan Dawson, an old Boys' Club stalwart and the doyen of schools football in the town, and Charlie Mills, a League official, were already in the middle when the coin was spun.

Jack Anderson won the toss for us and opted to bat first. The innings, as it turned out, proved uneventful and we made 163 for 5 in our 35 overs. I contributed a sprightly, if cross batted 19, at number six.

By now the crowd sprawled around the boundary had grown to a couple of hundred. I gave our fans something to cheer about when I clean bowled the number one and number three in successive overs. Ralph Dempster, as usual, was proving to be the stumbling block. He had his usual slow start taking no risks and shielding the new batsmen. The occasional four kept his side in touch with the scoring rate of just over five an over. I had been the steadier of our bowlers but was taken off with two of my allocation of ten overs remaining. Skipper Jack explained he wanted to keep them for a final fling later in the innings if needed. A whirlwind thirty from a middle order batsman who was dropped twice put North Blyth in with a chance. With three overs to go they wanted 13 with two wickets in hand and Ralphy Dempster, still keeping the innings together, on 71 not out. Jack threw the ball to me and I began to pace out my 25 yards run even though my mark from the first spell was still there. It was a habit and also a bit of gamesmanship, particularly against a number ten. I raced in at full pace and proceeded to knock the off stump out of the ground.

After the congratulations of my team mates had subsided I walked slowly back to my mark and turned only to find the arrival of the last man at the crease was being delayed by a lengthy discussion with Ralphy in the middle of the pitch. The tactics they had worked out became obvious when the number eleven advanced down the wicket, bat held high over his head, and let the ball strike his pads – a leg bye. A grinning Ralphy to face the strike. I started my run but had only gone five paces when Ralphy held up his hand and proceed to ask the umpire to check his middle and leg guard. I had already determined not to let anything Ralphy did put me off his game. But the batsman was equally determined and proceeded to block the next three fast and true deliveries with the solid face of the bat. The final ball of the over though was tickled to fine leg for a single. Twelve to win, two overs to go and Ralphy Dempster on strike. Now my bowling partner was not the most consistent as far as line and length was concerned but proceeded to deliver three beauties which shaved the off stump and went safely through to the keeper. It was not to last. Two successive long hops were despatched to the boundary. Four to win, seven balls to go.

The last ball of the over was swatted away to short mid-wicket for a single. Three to win – six balls to go. Me against Ralphy. I raced in and crashed a vicious delivery just short of a length. It failed to rise as high as it should and struck the North Blyth skipper in his most sensitive area. It was then we realised Ralphy did not use a box for batting either. His hiss of agony was followed by a slow Indian war dance around the stumps with his bat flung away in the direction of square leg to allow both hands to clutch the painful area. My team mates pounced on the ball, not that Ralphy was in any condition to run. He may have been in dire pain but he was making sure he kept in his crease. Within a couple of minutes, he resumed his stance. My second bouncer rose at the correct height and he ducked under it. He then just kept out the third ball, a yorker, which squirted away to be brilliantly fielded by second slip diving to his right. Three balls to go, three runs to get.

I was walking slowly back as the two batsmen huddled together in deep conversation in the middle of the pitch, Ralphy doing most of the talking. I arrived at my mark, waited until they had gone to their ends, turned and started to move forward. It was then Ralphy suddenly shouted, 'Run.' At that the two batsmen hared down the wicket to the opposite ends. I stopped in amazement.

'Don't be stupid,' I yelled. 'The ball isn't in play.' By this time the Ralphy was only a few yards from me having raced way past the stumps.

'Of course it is,' he said. 'You started your run.'

Ralphy turned to Dan Dawson, the Boys' Club umpire, for confirmation. 'I haven't a clue,' came the reply. Charlie Mills was just

Cecil Pearson (front row, second left) skippered Blyth first team during the 1965 season. He is pictured here outside the home dressing room at the Plessey Road ground with his side. Back row: Geoff Strong, Peter Robertson, Graham Heatley, Brian Storey, Frank Barker, John Cameron. Front row: Melvin Bruce, Cecil Pearson, Neil Mitcheson, Alan Harper and the author.

as non-plussed after being called across from square leg. The laughter and cheers of the North Blyth fans had by this time upset the Boys' Club supporters and furious arguments were raging. Some of the players were also involved until both skippers quietened them down. A suggestion that a check on the laws on the game in the back of the score book was of no help at all. The book gave the basic rules with no mention of when the ball was actually in play. Jack Anderson and the rest of us were adamant that the run should not count but Ralphy and his men stuck to their guns. The stand off lasted fifteen minutes before the two umpires got together and said in the interests of getting the game finished the run would be allowed but it was not to be repeated.

Two balls to go, two runs to win. I was absolutely seething as I went back to my mark. As I raced in Ralphy was in a pre-sprinting position to set off to the batting end come what may. My right arm came over as I leapt high but the ball somehow stayed in my hand. As I landed I skidded to a halt, turned and broke the wicket at my end. Ralphy was by this time ten yards down the track when the appeal for a run out went up. Dan Dawson looked at me and tut-tutted. 'Distinctly ungentlemanly conduct,' he said. 'But out.' And grinned as he lifted his finger to the sky.

Footnote: The Blyth Tradesman's League ran for several years in the 1950s with matches played by several teams on shared concrete wickets at the Isabella Colliery, Broadway and Cowpen. Several players in the league – the author, Ralphy, Bobby Cummings, Bobby Watson and Tommy Taylor – eventually graduated to play for Blyth Cricket Club.

It's Not Against The Rules

To the desperate sports editors that summer Saturday night in 1975 the arrival of a report on a cricket match on Tyneside was manna from the Gods. Their regional sports pages were crying out for local copy and there was none. Rain had washed out play before it began in every league from the Humber to the Cheviots and even further afield. The match played almost in the shadow of the huge shipbuilding cranes along the banks of the Tyne, was the only game in the whole of the North that day. And the prominence it was given the following morning on the back pages of the Sunday nationals showed how delighted the Fourth Estate was to have it. Little did those editors know though how close they were to having a piece of cricketing history to report.

The match in question was Percy Main against Blyth in the Northumberland League. 'Main' were well in the running for the championship and were breathing down the necks of the current champions and arch rivals, County Club. Blyth, on the other hand were once again seeking to avoid retaining the wooden spoon and were involved in a desperate battle for points with their rivals for the unwanted trophy – Backworth.

I was not only captain of the Blyth side but also number one chauffeur. When we set off on the nine miles trip with a full car load the skies were looking ominous. A dark grey mass had been gradually creeping down the North East coast from Scotland – the first threat of rain for over two weeks. As I pulled into the Percy Main car park the first spots struck the windscreen. By the time I had lifted the team bag out of the boot it was becoming insistent and had the bag not been so heavy I would have sprinted to the pavilion. My team-mates, ever the pessimists, left their gear in the car but brought their cards and liar dice with them ready for the long wait.

It was customary when rain prevented play starting, to wait a couple of hours, have an early tea, and then make a decision on abandoning the game. Such appeared to be the format facing the 22 players, two scorers and two umpires that afternoon. The card game was quickly started in the dressing room but I did not join in. Instead I borrowed a coat and walked out to survey the wicket. Despite the rain the cracks in the rolled surface were still there and I was unable to make an impression on the bone hard earth with my thumb. It was a match I

A familiar figure with his sketch pad and pipe on the North East cricket grounds was the Journal cartoonist Dudley Hallwood. He enjoyed his outings – and a couple of pints with the players after the match.

desperately wanted played as one point from a rained off game would do nothing for our precarious league position. Additionally Percy Main were always a side capable of a sudden collapse and being beaten despite having three county batsmen in their ranks.

As I walked slowly back to the pavilion I looked up at the flag pole and smiled. In pre-breathalyser days we had had many a fine night at the Percy Main bar and on one occasion Willie Mitcheson, our slow bowler and respected schoolteacher, had accepted a midnight bet to climb that very same flagpole. A foolish bid, as it turned out, for which he needed medical treatment. Poor Willie stripped to the waist – to save his shirt, he said – and left the pavilion. He returned with his chest torn and bleeding having forgotten in his semi-inebriated state that the first ten feet of the pole was encased in an old, terribly rusted, metal sheath. He had, according to witnesses, made six attempts to win the bet but failed each time to reach the wooden section of the pole.

To the right of the pavilion were the remains of the old toilet, a corrugated iron lean-to in which were deposited ashes and coke in a trough. The actual toilet was a small shed containing a portable loo

Cartoonist Dudley Hallwood was at the Morpeth-Blyth match to report the Northumberland League "derby."

The author was captured twice by Journal cartoonist Dudley Hallwood who was well aware of his guitar strumming antics.

wreaking of disinfectant. Soon it would all be different. A brand new pavilion was in course of erection. The foundations were already in and the scaffolding was in place.

My memories vanished as I turned my thoughts to the match and the points which could be ours. I decided to challenge the Percy Main skipper, Roy Jowsey, to start the game in the rain on the premise that the pitch was playable. It was an idea which got short thrift. 'We'll never get through 100 overs in that,' said Roy.

'Then how about a reduced overs game?' I asked.

Roy, never a one at a loss for words, replied, 'Divvent taak daft. We can't do that. The rules say 50 overs a side.'

'Not,' says I. 'If the side batting first declares, say after 25 overs.' Roy looked puzzled until I explained, 'If the side batting second fails to reach the total by the end of their 25th over then they declare as well. We'll have a match of two declarations with one team getting the five points.'

An astonished look appeared on Roy's face. 'It can't be done,' he spluttered.

I then played my trump card. 'Show me any law of cricket which says two sides cannot declare in a single innings match?'

'We'd never get away with it,' said Roy.

'We'll never know unless we try,' I replied.

The conversation was taking place on the veranda of the wooden pavilion out of the earshot of the other players. Roy looked thoughtful. 'I'll have to put it to the lads.' We then walked inside to confront our astonished teams.

As I expected, apart from one or two grumbles from senior players about getting soaked, we were all for it. Roy was finding it harder work facing fierce opposition particularly from Brian Newbold, his opening bowler, who said in no way was he going out into the rain. The gradual realisation that Percy Main could steal a march on County Club, if, as they confidently expected to, they won eventually brought him round. The problem of the two umpires, who, surprisingly were keen on the idea, was quickly resolved with the appearance of waterproof trousers and coats and the deal was struck. The all-important toss of the coin, with the loser batting first, took place. We would take first knock.

Years later my memory of the innings was that the pitch was still hard, I got an unbeaten fifty, ruined a pair of batting gloves and a cap and of the fielders vying for the position which allowed them to shelter under the scaffolding of the new pavilion. But the most vivid memory was the sight of the five stumps behind me as I crouched over my bat. The two extra were provided by a continuous stream of rain direct from the centre of both bails to the ground.

We were 127 for 5 at the end of the 25th over and the rain was still beating down. I was still batting so I turned to Roy at first slip and said, 'Right then, that's our knock over.' Tea was a steamy affair with the fielders drying off in the heat of the pavilion. I took Roy to one side and said, 'While I trust you like a brother, if you don't declare at the end of

25 overs I bring my team off.'

Roy replied, 'You have my solemn promise.'

It looked at one stage as if there were indeed going to be two declarations in a single innings game. Percy Main were slipping slightly behind the run rate for a while but as my fielders slithered and the bowlers lost their grip on the soggy ball the home batsmen were able to increase the tempo. With two overs to go they needed just seven with plenty of wickets in hand. This they achieved winning the game with six balls to spare and losing forever a place in cricketing history.

Footnote: The game created a furore in official league circles particularly from the County Club camp. But the result stood. Blyth finished bottom of the table but Percy Main failed to land the title.

A Duck to Dine On

There was no way in July 1970 that the chairman of Blyth Cricket Club could be a man lacking in mobility. The times when he was the respected figurehead, the motivator, not the doer, were long gone. But the glory days in the Northumberland League when the crowd stood and sat three or four deep and programmes were printed in their hundreds were in the past. So was the chairman's leisurely stroll around the boundary to receive the respectful acknowledgements of the spectators. The walk around the ground was now made for the prime purpose of selling raffle tickets for a bottle of wine or a box of chocolates to the fifty or so fans to help defray the cost of the umpires or the ball. While I was still a current first team player I was finding out that, in this day and age, chairman meant number one worker, principal grass cutter, pitch preparer, fund raiser, barman and on occasions tea-maker. As I sat on the roller preparing that afternoon's wicket I recalled the brief resurgence of interest in local cricket some years earlier when Rohan Kanhai was a professional in the league with Ashington.

What a draw and a moneymaker he proved as thousands of fans turned out around the county to watch him in action. So it was at Blyth when hundreds poured into the ground to see him.

An unfortunate decision by Bill Emery, the then Blyth skipper, ruined the day and the profits on the extra teas and the bar marquee. Bill was an enigma in that on one occasion he turned up for the opening match of the season with his old RAF haversack, took out his gear for the first time since the last match of the previous season and without having had one net pre-season hit a 50. Anyhow on the Kanhai occasion he won the toss and decided to the astonishment of his team, including me, to let Kanhai field. We were at that stage of the season vying for the league wooden spoon and it showed when we were skittled out for a paltry 57 in double quick time. Now a week earlier the West Indian star, who wrote a column in a local paper, implied that

The author skippered Blyth first team for three years in the 1960s. Here he is with his team, which on occasions included his younger brother Bill. Back row: Peter Robertson, Wilf Atkinson, Raymond Swann, Clive Page, Sid Moralee, Derek Denholm. Front row: Bill Harland, Frank Scott, the author, Neil Mitcheson, Graham Heatley.

umpires were biased in his favour so as not to disappoint the crowds he had been drawing. It was an opinion most teams in the league agreed with.

It so happened early in the Ashington chase for the 57 that Graham Heatley, the county fast bowler had Kanhai plumb leg before when he was in single figures. The deafening appeal was turned down much to the disgust of several of the fielding side – a number of whom were then threatened with being reported to the league for using foul and obscene language towards a match official. I was not one of them but I was fortunate the umpire was not a mind reader. Kanhai, to his credit, deliberately spooned the next ball he received into the air but it fell short of a fielder. Facing Cecil Pearson at the other end he did the same again and this time before it was even caught had set out for the pavilion.

As I chugged up and down the field on the cutter I reminisced on what this particular Saturday could have been for the Plessey Road Ground. The visitors were Percy Main who boasted the young Middlesex opening batsman and intellectual Mike Brearley. He did not have the pulling power of Kanhai but he was gathering a following and was hotly tipped as a potential England captain, eventually getting the job. The Main had acted quickly when they heard that Mike was to spend a year lecturing at Newcastle University. He accepted their offer to play league cricket when academic and first class cricket commitments allowed.

Unfortunately for Blyth, the University was down for the summer and Mike was in London playing for Middlesex. The chance of a big crowd and extra cash in the coffers was lost. Brearley had played two matches at Lords that week and made double figures on three occasions but no really big score.

With about 45 minutes to go to match time I garaged the cutter, jumped into my car and drove the mile home for a wash and a light lunch. To save time I changed into my cricket gear at home and headed back to the ground. Peter Robertson, our then captain, had already spun up and my team mates were out on the pitch preparing to field. Peter shouted, 'Open at the Plessey Road end.' There was no time for the usual welcoming courtesies to the visiting team as I laced up my boots before trotting out on to the field and pacing out my run.

The breeze was blowing across the pitch, an ideal aid to the away swinger I thought as I rubbed the virginal red and shiny ball on my right thigh. The two Percy Main openers were walking towards the wicket. I recognised one of them as a long-serving bat who had played in the minor counties competition but the other was a stranger.

I thought the fresh faced youngster was an up and coming second teamer promoted because of the absence of Brearley. I was still rubbing the ball at the end of my run when the two openers parted and the youngster headed for the receiving end. Confident young 'un, I thought, wanting to take the first ball of the game. I decided to stick with my idea of the away swinger and turned the seam of the ball towards second slip. I ran in, over came my arm, and the ball floated medium pace in the air. Sure enough the combination of shine and breeze began to swing it away from its line on the off stump. The young batsman stylishly moved across, bat and pad firmly together, to watch it safely past the stumps. It was when it pitched on a good length that the unexpected happened. The ball cut back from the off, missed the inside of the bat, flicked the pad and hit middle and leg stumps. I stood astonished with my hands on my hips as the youngster started off for the pavilion. It was the first time since junior cricket I had taken a wicket with my opening ball. In the meantime the rest of my team were dancing around like dervishes. Their reaction had me baffled but I continued to shake the preferred hands and wallowed in the smiles and congratulations. 'What a wicket to get,' said my skipper.

'Come on, he was only a kid,' I replied.

'Some kid,' came the retort, 'that was Mike Brearley.'

Footnote: Percy Main declared at 220-1 and beat us easily. I have dined out on that duck story ever since, vigorously denying all claims from Percy Main, not including the sporting Mike Brearley, that the ball had struck a small stone on the wicket. A stone on a good length is not difficult to spot – even by an amateur groundsman!

Several years after being bowled for a first ball duck by the author the England captain, Mike Brearley, was the chief guest at a quiz and social at his former club, Percy Main. The author was the quizmaster and renewed his acquaintance with the England batsman.

The author enjoys a convivial drink with Stan Levison and Tom Spencer, the two umpires at the Callers-Pegasus international matches. Stan and the author met many times on the cricket field as they were captains of Ashington and Blyth cricket teams in the Northumberland League. Tom who lives in Seaton Delaval stood in many international matches around the world.

The Blyth Phoenix Cricket Team

The Blyth Phoenix cricket team was an offshoot of the Blyth Phoenix Dramatic Society and played regular weekend matches up and down Northumberland and Durham.

On one occasion they travelled to Richmond in North Yorkshire to play a Sunday friendly. After scoring almost 200 runs in their innings the Phoenix had an early success when the author bowled their opening batsman for a duck. He walked off and came back on with his team captain who said, 'Let us have a look at the ball.' We showed them the shiny new ball. 'You can't play with that,' said the Tyke's captain. 'You have to play with the ball we used.' And so it was that the batsman who was bowled for a duck came back in and scored over 50 hitting the beat-up ball all around the ground. Many Yorkshire folk say we were conned and that there was no such rule.

I believe them!

Many of the team in this picture were at Richmond. Back row: Arthur Coleman (scorer) Eddie Legg, Don Christie, the author, Greg Cormack, John Anderson, William McAvoy (umpire). Front row: Benny Cobb, Stan Riddell, Jack Anderson, Jimmy Young, Jimmy Craft and Bill McCabe.

Size Ten Boots

While keen on soccer my centre of balance was all wrong and I had a kind of lumbering gate. Nevertheless I can boast, if that is the word, of playing in the Northern Alliance against a Newcastle United side. At the time I was a junior reporter on the *Morpeth Herald* but made an extra ten bob, that's 50 pence nowadays, covering the Morpeth Town home matches for the Saturday sports edition of the *Evening Chronicle*. On this occasion I was met at the entrance to the ground, which was then on Mitford Road, by the Town secretary, Ralphy Craik.

'What size boots do you take?' he asked.

'Why?' I replied.

'We're four players short and face a big fine from the league if we don't field a team,' he said.

'But I'm hopeless.'

'Never mind that. What size boots do you take?'

'I can't do it. I've got 50 words to phone to the *Chronicle* at half-time and then 150 words at full time.'

Not to be outdone Ralphy said, 'I'll take the notes, give them to you, and you can ring in on the club phone.'

So it was, wearing a pair of size 10 borrowed boots, I lined up at left fullback against the might of Newcastle United – a team which boasted several reserve team players and two schoolboy internationals.

In those days the ball was all leather – a 'caser' they were known as because they encased a bladder. The balls had a leather lace, which not

Bob Murray, the chairman of Sunderland Football Club, believes in good press relations and holds an annual 'bash' for the North East media. On one occasion it involved a penalty shoot-out competition on Roker Park. The competition highlight was when veteran journalist Arthur Appleton (front row, second left) was found hunting around on his hands and knees – he'd lost his hearing aid!

only made you see stars but also left an imprint and sometimes a scar when you were unfortunate to head the lace. The ball we were using in the match was so heavy that on the first occasion when I tried to clear my lines, with what I thought was a powerful kick, the ball travelled all of six yards.

We did not manage to score but they found the net 13 times. I can proudly boast that the right winger I was marking did not score. What I tend to keep quiet is that he sent over nine crosses which were neatly headed and driven past our keeper, another stand-in, by a budding star called Houlahan.

Ralphy's association with Morpeth Town lasted over 40 years and a fitting tribute to him is that the new ground to the south of the town is known as Ralph Craik Memorial Park.

Whistle Blower

My soccer interest was not just in watching and reporting. I took time out to qualify as a Class One soccer referee. While I would have loved to have made the Football League list I started too late in life and contented myself with refereeing in the Blyth and District Sunday League which was run by Alan Davison who also found time to control the youngsters in the Blyth Hearts Juvenile Jazz Band.

When working on newspapers, I occasionally had a Saturday afternoon off which meant I could make myself available at short notice to the Northumberland Referees Pool. This meant I could be allocated a match at a couple of hours notice anywhere on Tyneside or in Northumberland. It is with some regret the number of Saturday leagues is dwindling. At one time all the Blyth council soccer pitches at Broadway, Cowpen, Newsham and Isabella were in use but now they are desolate just waiting for the Sunday teams to turn out.

The highlight of my ten-year refereeing career was when George Watson, the secretary of Blyth Spartans, invited me to referee the Spartans against Sunderland in a pre-season friendly at Croft Park. Sunderland sent their first team and there were several thousand in the ground to watch the game. The two sets of players were not the only ones trying to get match fit and I was blowing like the proverbially winded cuddy after only ten minutes. Fortunately the teams slowed down and instead of route one to goal – up and over – started playing across the park. It was quite enjoyable even the humorous shouted references to my toupee from those in the know and those who guessed. After the match I approached George and asked him for my fee.

'Fee?' he retorted. 'Fee? Whey you dee this match for the honour.'

George, canny lad in both senses of the word, was deservedly appointed to the Northumberland FA. Rightly so for the time and effort he spent in helping to sustain and improve the reputation of the famous giant-killers and soccer in general.

The Cup Was Overflowing

The crate of bottled Federation Special – favourite beer of working men's clubs and House of Commons bars – was already tucked into the boot of the car along with what appeared to be half a ton of home made sandwiches as I set off to collect my pal Alf Douglas for the trip to Newcastle. Sure enough Alf, when he came to the door, was wearing the agreed uniform, a black and white bedecked boater, white cricket sweater, white shirt, black trousers and, of course, a huge rosette pinned to his left breast bearing the words, 'Howay Newcassel'.

For both of us it was to be our first trip to Wembley to see our favourite team. It was almost 20 years since the Magpies last appeared at the soccer mecca and this Saturday they were to take on the mighty Liverpool in the 1974 FA Cup Final.

It was just after seven on a cloudless, sunny morning, as I drove towards the city. The excursion train was due to leave the Central Station at eight and we would reach Wembley Station at half past twelve. A leisurely stroll up Wembley Way would then get us into the stadium well before kick-off. I slapped my breast pocket for the umpteenth time to check that I had the two tickets for the standing end opposite the players tunnel. 'God, I thought I'd lost them,' I joked. Alf grinned.

There was ample free parking space in the city at that time of morning and we had no difficulty finding a spot close to the station. It was already warm and the forecast was an even warmer day in the

Alf Douglas and the author who found themselves in deep water on their trip to the FA Cup Final at Wembley.

London area. I suggested, and Alf agreed, that we leave our jackets in the boot of the car and travel in our sweaters. I took the precious match and train tickets out of my coat and slipped them into the back pocket of my trousers, making sure the button was fastened properly. We piled the packs of corned beef and cheese and pickle sandwiches on top of the beer crate for the short walk through the majestically ornate Central Station portico. The queue for the soccer special train was already snaking 100 yards around the concourse. We joined the end of it, bidding the two fresh faced teenagers ahead of us a hearty, 'Wot Cheor,' as we lowered our crate of liquid refreshment to the ground.

Even at that time of morning the atmosphere was tremendous, full of anticipation of a great game ending, naturally, in a Newcastle victory. After all the Geordies had 'Supermac' – Malcolm Macdonald, wearing the number nine shirt and upholding in fine style the striking traditions of Jackie Milburn and Hughie Gallagher. And hadn't he scored a hat-trick against the very same side on his debut for Newcastle? Everyone agreed that if the team played as well as it had in the semi-final at Hillsborough then the Scousers – Kevin Keegan and all – would not stand a chance.

I was beginning to regret leaving my jacket in the car. I felt the precious match tickets were extremely vulnerable in my back pocket – particularly when, as I had been warned, light fingered cockney Fagins lurked virtually on every corner in London on cup final day. It would be unbearable being stranded outside the twin towers as the lads marched to victory inside.

'Why don't I keep them in my shoe that would seem to be the safest spot,' I suggested to Alf. He agreed and the precious two bits of paper were soon in the white cricket sock on my left foot. 'I feel a lot happier now,' I said, stamping my foot on the ground to test it for comfort. It was then the giant black and white snake, now threading its way out into the station portico, began to ease forward through the gates and over the hump-backed bridge to the soccer special standing on the other side of the track. Thankfully there was no mad rush as the organisers had allocated reserved seats for everyone. For this I was grateful as the crate of Fed Special, now dangling between me and Alf, could have come to an unthinkable and undrinkable end.

We found our seats without much difficulty and stowed the crate and sandwiches under the table in front of us. It did not take long for the 500 fans to clamber aboard and the train soon moved slowly out of the station over the River Tyne on its way south. The first bottles of Fed Special were opened before the train passed through Durham. We were both sampling the first mouthfuls when two supporters club train marshals entered the carriage urging fans to check they had their match tickets.

'It looks,' says I, taking the bottle from my lips. 'As if some stupid idiot has lost his ticket.'

'Just as well we've got ours,' replied Alf.

At this I reached down to my left ankle for a reassuring check. The look of panic on my face implied something was wrong. 'Stop kidding,' said Alf. 'Show me the tickets.'

I kicked off my shoe and just as quickly slipped it back on saying, 'I'll be back in a minute.'

At this I rose and pursued the two marshals into the next carriage. The smile on my face when I returned a couple of minutes later told Alf everything he wanted to know. The tickets had been found lying on the footbridge leading to the train having worked their way out of the sock. Thankfully I was able to identify them by giving them the letter of the section of the ground they had been issued for. Stunned silence followed for a few moments as we contemplated what might have been and tried to work out how the tickets could have moved from inside the shoe, up the sock, and on to the ground.

'The chap who found them is two carriages up,' I told Alf. 'I think we should thank him.'

One of the marshals pointed out the middle aged fan who acknowledged our grateful thanks, spurned a cash reward but willingly accepted a couple of bottles of Fed. The rest of the journey was

When someone remarked that the comic figure about to be used by Blyth Valley Council in 1983 to promote cleanliness in the town looked just like Alf Douglas he was called in to launch the campaign. He is seen here with the Mayor at the time, Councillor Derek Raffle and Derek's mother.

uneventful. By the time the train pulled into Wembley Station the beer, and most of the sandwiches had been consumed. We followed the crowd towards the mecca of English soccer and wallowed in the atmosphere of Wembley Way and the sight of the twin towers, the fluttering flags and the hundreds of multi-coloured luxury coaches in the huge bus parks.

I had the tickets clutched in my hand inside my trouser pocket as we hunted for the correct turnstile and it was with relief I handed them over to the attendant. Our section was tucked well under the stand at least fifty yards away from the nearest sunlight and with absolutely no chance of our spouses back on Tyneside fulfilling their promises of spotting us on television. Being over six foot tall we both opted to give smaller fans a chance by standing on the last step before the concreted alley which ran around the back of the stand. We cheered on that other Geordie hero and staunch Newcastle supporter, Brendan Foster, as he won a 5,000 metre challenge race as a prelude to the final. It was after this we made our fatal mistake.

One fan, who had made his way up from the depths of the crowd behind the goals, asked us for directions to the nearest toilet. As it so happens it was quite a distance away. We did point out the concrete wall a couple of yards away on the other side of the alley could serve a similar purpose and save him a long walk in the bargain. He gratefully took our advice. We were soon to find out the fan, rather like an ant on a scouting mission, had hundreds of friends also seeking a handy toilet. Within a couple of minutes both of us, and all those around us, found ourselves standing in the middle of a wide stream of waste water cascading down the terrace steps. The flows eased at kick-off but resumed at half-time.

Now standing in pools of filtered water is bad enough but watching your side trounced in the bargain is purgatory. Newcastle were being massacred. Two goals by Kevin Keegan, later to become a Geordie hero himself, elicited groans from the fans. Supermac, the hero of Tyneside, had a stinker. His one shot in the whole game was so far off target it was unbelievable. For both of us the final whistle could not come early enough. With Geordie politeness we applauded as Liverpool walked up the steps to the Royal Box to receive the trophy but left before the Reds took their lap of honour.

We sat on a wall in Wembley Way dangling our bare feet as we tried to dry off our socks and shoes before heading for the train. Black and White rosettes were being dropped to the ground in their scores and a number of scarves met the same fate. It was only after a quiet and rather dismal journey home the humour of the situation dawned on us as we began to walk wearily from the Central Station. It was a passing United fan who started us off. To his astonishment we burst into laughter after he said, 'We must have been mad. Fancy travelling all the way down there to be well and truly pissed on.'

SECTION NINE

AND FINALLY ...
MUSIC, MUSIC, MUSIC

During a spell on the Cambridge Evening News in 1955 the author was resident vocalist with the Vince Wright Orchestra at the Rex Ballroom in the university city. On one occasion the internationally famous Ted Heath brought his band to the Rex and the Wright orchestra, and vocalist, found themselves using the Ted Heath stands during an interval break. Fame at last!

It must be obvious if you have ploughed through the book that music has played a large part in the life of your author.

There has been brief mention of my singing career – the Roxy Ballroom at Blyth, the Rex Ballroom in Cambridge and my life on the amateur musical stage.

What I have omitted is my twelve month career as the leader of a skiffle group in and around Blyth.

It came about in 1956 when skiffle – Lonnie Donegan, Nancy Whiskey, et al ruled the charts.

Tea chest basses – string knotted through the hole in the bottom of the chest and attached to a broom handle - were becoming the rage as were metallic wash boards, which could produce a great rhythm.

My old friend, Alf Douglas was on the tea chest moving the broom handle backward and forward to alter the tone of the notes as he plucked it. Dave Armstrong, now a respected church organist in the town, played piano. Lol Hepple whose contribution was very athletic dancing in the modern style. Arthur Brown who sang and played biscuit tin with me as the lead singer doubling also on washboard.

Put the five together and 'The Rollin Rockers' were born and believe it or not social clubs were prepared to pay to hear our offerings.

The first was the North Blyth BRSA Social Club. I was offered a fee of £5 to take the group over the chain ferry to the drinking establishment. We had no transport so we carried the tea chest bass and the biscuit tins through the town and to the boat.

With a programme of only eight numbers we thought we might be in trouble but we went down a storm with the audience not bothered about us encoring the songs over and over. Indeed we were rebooked at the club during the interval.

Realising we really lacked proper musical ability I told the group the £5 was going to be invested in two guitars. And so it was I travelled by bus to Newcastle and bought two Spanish style guitars and two tuition books – all for the five pounds!

I handed one guitar and book to Arthur with instructions to learn three basic chords in time for our next booking at the Seaton Terrace. For the next week I locked myself in the bathroom at home and after mastering the tuning of the instrument sat strumming the three chords for hours on end.

I must say by the time our next booking came around I was proficient enough with only the three chords to contribute some backing to our numbers.

The booking was at the High Street Social Club in Blyth, then a rather small place compared to the establishment that exists nowadays. We got set up and launched into our first number *Freight Train* – the Nancy Whiskey hit. While I may not have been completely in tune with the piano it did not seem too bad. But it was Arthur on his guitar who had me puzzled. He had it slung around his neck and appeared by the rapid movement of his fingers to be using every fret with astonishing dexterity.

At the end of the number I said to him, 'Very impressive Arthur but I did not hear a note from you.'

'Yes, well,' says Arthur. 'I just couldn't understand the book!'

Needless to say Arthur was back on biscuit tin the next booking. And there were certainly plenty of those for the Rollin Rockers. We travelled up and down Northumberland and on occasions in Durham. After a year, however, the group came to a sudden end when the Tax Man pounced.

We all had to fork out about six pounds each in back payments.

It did not, however, stop yours truly from entertaining because the Alf and Jim Duo – Alf Douglas and your author – came into being.

We found our mix of comedy magic, straight singing and comedy duos – to be highly popular at dinners, cabarets and Masonic socials. But we learned very quickly that our entertainment was not of the type required by hardened social club goers. A couple of early bookings taught us that lesson.

So it was with some reservations that we agreed to be supporting acts to Nola, a professional London singer, who was spending the Christmas holidays with my sister-in-law in Blyth.

Nola had asked me to get her a couple of bookings while she was in the North East and I fixed her up at the Waterloo Social Club in Blyth and at the New Hartley Social Club. And it was at New Hartley, where our mutual pal Brian Lambert was the resident accompanist, that they

The Blyth Magic Circle flourished for many years in the town and even ran a junior section. Unfortunately the number of enthusiasts for the skill dwindled and it went out of existence in the mid-1980s. The annual dinner and competition in the North Blyth BRSA Club, known locally as The Bandroom, was the highlight of the year. Seen here are, from left to right: Alan Bell, Dennis Crozier, Alf Douglas, Tommy Aldus, John Bell, Jim Leslie, George Elliott and Bill Elliott (no relation). Membership of the Magic Circle meant unintentional fame as a comedy magician for Alf Douglas. He prepared a serious act for the annual competition and when all the tricks went wrong to roars of laughter from the audience he decided to continue in the Tommy Cooper vein. The highly popular act has taken him to hundreds of venues throughout the North East and further afield.

wanted the supporting acts.

I opened up with three songs from the shows, which did not go down too badly, and then Alf went on for his first spot. It was a disaster. Comedy magic was not to the taste of the New Hartleyites and he cut the act short.

Coming off stage he declared he was not doing a second spot. In the meantime Nola was going great guns and had the entire room on her side.

The second act started again with me singing three songs. I came off to find Alf was still not happy about going on again. Somehow we managed to persuade him and he went on to the strains of the *Dead March* from Saul played by a grinning Brian Lambert!

Again the act flopped but, encouraged by cries of 'Keep going' from the wings, he managed to stay on longer.

Now Alf and I were double booked that night and were due to do a ten-thirty cabaret spot at the Ashington Hirst Welfare for a private dinner-dance. So while Nola again took the New Hartley club by storm we headed for Ashington.

Alf, with exactly the same act that flopped at New Hartley, received a standing ovation at Ashington!

It was some time before we succumbed to another social club booking but after we had performed at a dinner at Whitley Bay we were approached by a man who said he was an official at Swarland Social Club up near Alnwick.

We were, he said, just the act that would go down well at his club. Despite our protestations he insisted we would do well and in the end we agreed.

And so it was we arrived at a rather comfortable-looking single storeyed building, which made up the Swarland Social Club. There was a good crowd in of middle-aged and elderly members, men and women, as we set up our equipment.

The chairman announced us and off we went with our opening duets which usually got a laugh as we clowned on. On this occasion they didn't. I sang a couple of songs, which did not go down too badly, and then Alf came on for his spot.

The cries of 'Keep going' again rang out from the wings and we eventually brought the first half to a close. As we sat in the dressing room the chairman came in. He pointed at Alf and said, 'Don't bother going on in the second half.' He then turned to me and said, 'Do you sing rock and roll?'

I told him unless we both went on neither of us would.

'Fair enough,' said the chairman. 'I'm paying you off. We'll get Jackie up on his mouth organ – he can play rock and roll.'

Now to get to the dressing rooms you had to walk the full length of the club and neither of us fancied facing the embarrassment of lugging our gear back the way we came. We ended up lowering the gear out of the window on to an outside path, nonchalantly sauntering down the room as if going to the bar and killing ourselves with laughter as we drove home. We never did meet up again with that official who booked us. Needless to say from that time on we stuck to our principle of avoiding social clubs like the plague despite what was offered.

Now hotels were a different kettle of fish and we accepted a booking for a dinner at an hotel in Stamfordham. It was deep into winter and while there was no snow around there certainly was plenty of frost. Alf owned a grey Ford Capri which we used to travel into the heart of Northumberland for the gig.

We had a great night and on coming out Alf found he could not open the car door. 'It's the frost,' he said. 'It's frozen solid.'

We pondered for a while then I suggested hot water would free the lock. But where to get it? As we both had had a couple of pints during the evening the solution was simple.

Alf had just got down to it when there came a shout from a man leaving the hotel about thirty yards away, 'Hey, what are you doing with my car?'

Sure enough another grey Capri – Alf's – was a couple of cars away down the car park.

Fortunately we managed to meet the driver half way and explain the error before he discovered he had a wet and smelly driver's door!

Alf readily admits that in his younger days he had a foot infection problem, which made enclosed quarters a rather smelly business. Now Peter Robertson, my opening bowling pal at Blyth, had the same problem but even worse.

It so happened we were booked to entertain at a dinner at the Queens Head in Morpeth and Peter was to be our accompanist. I was to be the chauffeur that night and was not looking forward to driving the pair home after they had been cooped up in a very warm function room at the hotel.

So that is how the pair of them sat in the back of the car from Morpeth to Blyth with their feet stuck out of the rear windows!

During the following cricket season Peter burst in to our dressing room at Blyth to announce he had the cure for his foot problem. Up to this time he had been forced by a unanimous vote of his team-mates to change into his boots either in the shower or outside in the fresh air.

Peter then opened up a pack of shoe insoles which claimed they just ate up the odours. They were new on the market, Peter said, and proceeded to put them inside his boots.

We fielded first and Peter bowled his usual ten to fifteen overs. It was when we returned to the pavilion for tea he removed his boots in the shower then began laughing. He came into the dressing room holding two tattered and smelly insoles in his hands.

'They've surrendered,' he said.

I am delighted to say that both Alf and Peter have overcome their foot problems and have indeed since travelled in my car with their feet inside the vehicle.

And that, dear reader, is where we leave you. I do hope you have enjoyed my reminiscences, all of which were most definitely TRUE.

The author, his wife Rosemary, with daughters Janet (left) and Alison pictured in the garden of their Blyth home on the occasion of his 65th birthday.

The People's History

To receive a catalogue of our latest titles send a large SAE to:

The People's History
Suite 1
Byron House
Seaham Grange Business Park
Seaham
County Durham
SR7 0PY

www.thepeopleshistory.co.uk